WE CARRY THE F/RE

Family and Citizenship as Spiritual Calling

WE CARRY THE F RE

Family and Citizenship as Spiritual Calling

RICHARD A. HOEHN

CHURCH
PUBLISHING
INCORPORATED

Unless otherwise noted, the Scripture quotations are from New Revised Standard Version Bible, copyright © 1989 National Council of the Churches of Christ in the United States of America. Used by permission. All rights reserved worldwide.

An earlier version of "We Worked for Changes" appeared as "Praxis Education for Justice" in *Academy*, XLI: 3/4 (1985). An earlier version of "The More 'Other,' the More We Can Learn" was published as "I'm Here" in *The Lutheran*, March 6, 1985.

"Those Who Give Light" (page 24), "The Silent Seduction of Social Media" (page 51), "Nine Kitchen Matches" (page 79), "A Suicide Note from Democracy" (page 101), "E-mail Sonnet for My Mother" (page 127), "A Reply from My Mother" (page 127), "In the Plaza" (page 133), "The Sun Rises Like Fire" (page 150), "One Pale Blue Drop, Falling" (page 175), "The Firebird" (page 198), "The Secret" (page 224), and "ain't done" (page 229) copyright © Jim Benton. Used by permission.

Church Publishing
19 East 34th Street
New York, NY 10016
www.churchpublishing.org

Cover design by Marc Whitaker, MTWdesign
Typeset by Rose Design

Library of Congress Cataloging-in-Publication Data

Names: Hoehn, Richard A., 1936- author.
Title: We carry the fire : family and citizenship as spiritual calling / Richard A. Hoehn.
Identifiers: LCCN 2020040677 (print) | LCCN 2020040678 (ebook) | ISBN 9781640653825 (paperback) | ISBN 9781640653832 (epub)
Subjects: LCSH: Service (Theology) | Vocation--Christianity. | Christian sociology.
Classification: LCC BT738.4 .H64 2021 (print) | LCC BT738.4 (ebook) | DDC 261.8/3--dc23
LC record available at https://lccn.loc.gov/2020040677
LC ebook record available at https://lccn.loc.gov/2020040678

To my wife Carole Zimmerman
for her steadfast love and support.

To our children Christine J. Hoehn, Thomas A. Hoehn,
Karen E. Hoehn, Benjamin Douglass Hoehn, Kristin N. Sizemore;
their respective partners Chelsey Bobbe, Juan Russo,
Craig Winneker, Yongsun Lee, Gregory Ballheim;
and our grandchildren
Rosalind Joyce Winneker and Jasung Albert Hoehn.

Contents

Preface

Famous Brazilian author Joaquim Maria Machado de Assis described the idea for *The Posthumous Memoirs of Brás Cubas* as something hanging from a trapeze in his brain for a long time before he was able to articulate that idea and write it down. So it has been with *We Carry the Fire*: the initial intuition jumped onto a trapeze in my head thirty years ago. I was doing grassroots organizing with member-activists of Bread for the World, whose family-and-citizen spirituality was different than most popular, and many sanctioned, spiritualities. The idea swung back and forth, touching ground and pushing off many times before maturing and landing here.

Popular spiritualities say, "Go on a retreat, meditate, seek a guru, study religious texts" for personal peace, insight, and salvation. We often feel a need for rebalancing, healing, insight, and respite from the clamor, pressures, and troubles of everyday life. However, it is also urgent (I would say *more* urgent) that we create the conditions that undergird the possibility of retreats and meditations—by mitigating pandemics, tyrannies, wars, and environmental catastrophes that do violence to individuals and families.

In popular spiritualities, almost anything pushes people's spiritual buttons—worship, crystals, tai chi, candlelight, drugs, retreats, whipping yourself on the back until you bleed. Meanwhile, the life blood of families and the planet flows out in trickles and torrents. How is it even possible to find serenity in a world where someone dies in a war every minute, where there are twenty-seven cases of human trafficking, where more than 21,000 people die of hunger and hunger-related causes every day, and where climate change threatens all? Deep spirituality is best found when we are part of the worldwide family of sisters and brothers who are called to help move the human spirit forward.

We Carry the Fire offers a twenty-first-century social, political, and congregational spirituality that begins with actions that help restore families, communities, and the earth (*tikkun olam*). This spiritual calling has tangible outcomes in the real world, as John F. Kennedy said: "After the dust of the centuries have passed over our cities, we will be remembered not for our victories and defeats, but our contribution to the human spirit."

Since 1990, more than one billion people have been lifted out of extreme poverty, the global under-five mortality rate has declined by more than half, and 2.6 billion people have gained access to improved drinking water. These pre-COVID-19 gains represent an objective increase in the human spirit brought about by people who, though mostly unknown to one another and often at great personal sacrifice, worked to save lives and the planet.

When we actively engage in these efforts, we can experience a profound sense of spiritual meaning as we link our lives with humanity's deepest values and highest hopes in concert with people of every kind, in every place, on every day, all over the world. What greater spiritual activity is there than this?

We Carry the Fire is a positive message for all points on the right–left political spectrum, because the future lies in our shared agreement to support families, to work hard for what we believe in on all sides, to respect our personal and policy differences, and to negotiate the outcomes through democratic practices. We need a charitable politics in which we respect one another yet fight hard for our beliefs, a politics that is wise as serpents and gentle as doves, Martin Luther King's "tough mind and a tender heart."

The spirituality of *We Carry the Fire* is primarily about what you can give and only secondarily about the good feeling you can get. Fire spirituality is sparked by a realistic reading of the human condition that faces outward rather than inward; is self-consciously social, moral, and political; offers insight, strength, and hope for the future; a sense of connectedness and involvement; and is transformative for both recipients and doers. If you are one of those who carry the fire, your self-identity and social relationships will change, but what counts even more is that you will help change (dare I say, help *save*) the world.

But, you cannot do it alone. It takes a lot of us *working together* to accomplish these changes.

We Carry the Fire is based on real-life stories with existential authenticity, enriched by insights from social science, philosophy, and the arts—the latter because they illumine life's realities and possibilities in revealing and compelling ways. Literary critic John Gardner observed that art "clarifies life, establishes models of human action, casts nets toward the future, carefully judges our right and wrong directions, celebrates and mourns."[1] He added that the arts create "myths a society can live instead of die by" and "clearly our society is in need of such myths."[2] Ayn Rand's novels influenced more people than her treatises.

When Francisco Goya's servant asked why he did sketches of the barbarities they had seen during the Napoleonic invasion of Spain, Goya answered, "To have the pleasure of saying eternally to men that they stop being barbarians."[3] When asked by *The Los Angeles Times* to "describe the urge to write," noted author Harlan Ellison responded, "You do it to make a difference, to say, 'I was here. I was a force for good in some way.'"[4]

We Carry the Fire is written for people of faith and people with no definable faith because we all need meaningful practices that enlarge humanity and respect the planet—practices that reflect vision and commitment, the spirit of people of all nations, races, creeds, and languages; that exemplify the human desire for a better world that we all share; that say "I was here. I was a force for good in some way."

I write primarily from a background in Euro-American culture. I show respect for other traditions by not attempting the half-baked

1. John Gardner, *On Moral Fiction* (New York: Basic Books 1978), 100. "The arts provide a 'phenomenology of the soul,'" Gaston Bachelard, *The Poetics of Space* (Boston: Beacon, 1969), xvi.

2. Ibid., 126.

3. Charles Poore, *Goya* (New York: Charles Scribner's Sons, 1938), 178.

4. Matt Schudel, "Pugnacious Writer of Science Fiction," *Washington Post Obituaries,* July 1, 2018, C7.

descriptions we so often read. Wisdom and devotion exist wherever humans do. Our knowledge is limited, people have diverse experiences, and who knows what the future has to offer?

• • •

More than half a century ago, my first English assignment at Capital University was to write a five-page paper on any topic. I laboriously pecked out "The Meaning of Life" on my 1950s portable Underwood, ignorant of Dag Hammarskjöld's, "When a 17-year-old speaks [of the meaning of life], he is ridiculous, because he has no idea of what he is talking about."[5] Professor David Owens shared Hammarskjöld's sensibility. Handing the essay back, he grinned, and in his androgynous lilt advised, "Read some pulp fiction before you write a second draft."

I have wrestled with religious institutions, politics, spirituality, theology, ethics, justice, values, and the meaning of life in marriage and as a single parent, from the pew and pulpit, as student and professor, local activist and grassroots organizer, policy wink (not quite a wonk), and institute director working with nonprofits and official agencies in the United States and abroad. I have watched *Pulp Fiction, Pulp Fiction Art*, and *The Adventures of George the Projectionist* (a comedic combination of *Cinema Paradiso* and *Pulp Fiction*).

So, Professor Owens, wherever you are eating apple pie in the sky, here is my final draft. I am emboldened to write in the faith that most of us desire more robust family and civic lives that are safer, saner, more satisfying, beautiful, sustainable, just, peaceable, and also more spiritual.

---

5. Matt Fitzgerald and Christian Wiman, "Embrace and Abandonment: A Pastor and a Poet Talk about God," *Christian Century*, June 12, 2013, 22, https://www.christiancentury. org/article/2013-05/embrace-abandonment?reload=1592846492902.

Acknowledgments

Special thanks to Carole Zimmerman and Jim Benton for their editorial assistance and Jim for his poems, as well as to Patricia E. Meyers, Jim and Kathleen Sullivan Rurak, Benjamin Douglass Hoehn, and the anonymous author of "The Spirit of Goddess Was with Us" for allowing their personal stories to be included.

Thanks also to John Badertscher, Peter Bastien, Jud Dolphin, Karen Hoehn, Robin Hoover, and Chuck Melchert for helpful comments on early versions of the manuscript; Bread for the World and Bread for the World Institute members and staff with whom I served; and the members of Good Shepherd Lutheran Church (Brunswick, ME), Luther Place Memorial Church (DC), Christ the Servant Lutheran Church (Montgomery Village, MD), and Hope Lutheran Church (College Park, MD), who inspired chapters 7 and 8.

—RAH, Ash Wednesday, 2021

From the lectionary for the day:

> Is not this the fast that I choose:
>> to loose the bonds of injustice,
>> to undo the thongs of the yoke,
> to let the oppressed go free,
>> and to break every yoke?
> Is it not to share your bread with the hungry,
>> and bring the homeless poor into your house;
> when you see the naked, to cover them,
>> and not to hide yourself from your own kin?
> Then your light shall break forth like the dawn,
>> and your healing shall spring up quickly.

—Isaiah 58:6–8

Part I

Fire Spirituality

CHAPTER 1

The Fire We Carry, Carries Us

Transformative spirituality is a "life-energy." It is a breath of fire . . . an ember that sustains the flame of one's heart. It . . . calls the person to go beyond oneself, to concern for, and relationships with, the others. . . . finding the truth of one's existence and discovering the fire within . . . to be in solidarity with the poor in their struggle for freedom from all forms of unjust systems and structures present in society.

—*Dr. Rico Palaca Ponce, Institute of Spirituality in Asia*[1]

Embers, Flames, Extinguishers

In Cormac McCarthy's Pulitzer Prize–winning novel *The Road*, a father and son struggle to hold onto their lives and values in a dystopian future. They search for food, avoid predatory thugs, and see a "corpse in a doorway dried to leather" as they head south in freezing weather. The normal trappings of organized polite and policed civilization are gone. Their wife and mother, drained by their untenable situation and believing that all three of them would likely be raped, murdered, and eaten if they headed south, had committed suicide.

The father and son enter a house, open a trapdoor, and see emaciated human beings imprisoned alive for future consumption by a gang of hunters who are soon to return. The father assures his son, "We don't eat people. We are the good guys. We carry the fire." They flee, yet again, as the father protects and sacrifices for his son. The son trusts his father.

---

1. "Transformative Spirituality Is a Breath of Fire," World Council of Churches, March 23, 2012, *http://www.oikoumene.org/en/press-centre/news/transformative-spirituality-is-a-breath-of-fire.*

They eventually arrive at a coastline where the father succumbs to wounds and deprivation. The boy wanders alone. On the third day, he encounters a family.[2] The boy asks if they eat people. They say no. Then he asks if they carry the fire, vaguely aware that it means something like "Are you the good guys? Do you practice civilized values?" At first, they are unsure what "carrying the fire" means, but then answer "yes." They unite to become a new family, pilgrims traveling together toward an uncertain future.

Rico Palaca Ponce's call to discover "the fire within" is an articulation of "how to be a follower of Christ in today's context." Fire is also one of the great metaphors of classical mythologies, along with earth, air, and water. When Zeus withholds fire from humanity, Prometheus, the shaper, protector, and champion of people, steals the fire and gives it to humanity who use it to develop, and sometimes harm, civilization. Prometheus is also known as the father of the arts and sciences which is pertinent to our discussion here.

In the Bible, God destroys Sodom and Gomorrah with fire, appears to Moses in a burning bush, leads the people of Israel with a pillar of fire at night, and sends the Spirit as tongues of fire at Pentecost to empower the crowd to go forth and spread good news.

The myth of the firebird in both Eastern and Western culture typically involves a lengthy quest that has great promise, but also hardship and danger. The colorful Phoenix symbolizes rebirth. It lives, dies, then rises out of the ashes to live again. Funerary events in India and Indonesia sometimes include dramatic fire rituals.

It is not surprising that fire has played a significant role in the language and experience of spirituality. Fire is the mesmerizing mystery of dancing flame; smoke rising skyward and disappearing above like fading spirits; burning, consuming, destroying (sacrificial altars, St. Joan, witches, the KKK, torture, hell); but also lighting the path ahead, protecting from the hidden dangers of darkness, campfire camaraderie,

---

2. The father gives up his life for his son, and the three days reflect the Good Friday to Easter Sunday cycle in the church year.

and ghost stories; even cleansing and cauterizing. It goes cold and dies if it is not protected, rekindled, and tended.

In *The Road*, "carrying the fire" seems to mean "to support one another as family and press forward with civilized, humane values." People carry the fire in many places and in many ways. The focus in this book is on families, the public sphere, and congregations. Reforming addicts who have experienced personal dystopias tell us that when you face disaster, it is important to walk forward with the support of others—in their case, NA/AA families.

The COVID-19 crisis vividly demonstrated our need for other people, whether through the experience of being socially isolated or sick in hospitals. And it has freshened our awareness of the importance of political decisions for our daily lives—at its most dramatic, fewer or more people die depending on the decisions of political leaders.

The father and son in *The Road* never have personal names. They are, in any given moment, us. Life is already deeply dystopian for the people in the world who suffer oppression and injustice. Climate change threatens an engulfing chaos that some say is the end of civilization for all. No life is without trauma or existential threat.

Innumerable people throw water on the fire of our responsibility to live toward civilization's highest values, believing that their self-interest is the only thing that counts. Healthy self-interest is good, but when self-interest becomes a consuming selfishness, it scorches souls and leads people to oppress others.

The great majority of people have ambivalent embers that glow and dim, that need warming and tending to burn brightly. Families, congregations, and society provide the kindling. *We Carry the Fire* provides a little oxygen. It is up to you to help carry the fire that keeps our civilization's best values alight and alive.

In 1948, member countries of the United Nations General Assembly approved a shared commitment to fundamental human rights: the Universal Declaration of Human Rights. The Declaration was an expression of basic human values that underlie the protection and enhancement of civilized life. Nations came together across lines that normally separate and divide people and committed to a more moral human future.

In 2015, the United Nations Assembly went beyond rights and approved seventeen Sustainable Development Goals as a substantive expression of humanity's highest hopes. People of 193 nations—all creeds, races, religions, and regions of the world—committed to address the world's biggest concerns. The Global Goals represent a shared vision of a peaceful, plentiful, just, and sustainable world where the human spirit can thrive.[3]

The Declaration and the Goals are hugely important, but meaningless unless underlying social and political structures affirm and actively pursue them. Families, political systems, the arts, and religious congregations have historically been among those structures. At their best, they sort, preserve, teach, and model the core values and practices that have risen out of long-term human experience.

Grassroots on Fire

I worked at Bread for the World (BFW) and the Bread for the World Institute for seventeen years, beginning in 1988. There I encountered people in the United States and around the world who were fire-carrying practitioners. BFW staff and members around the country lobby Congress for policies that help people who are hungry and poor, both at home and abroad.

The staff made substantial sacrifices of income and time to work for and with poor people. It felt good, morally good, to be making a difference with my life, however small my individual impact. And it felt good, spiritually good, to be working in solidarity with other people in the office, around the country, and around the world who were committed to share the warmth—the fire of our joint actions—to implement humane values, help families, promote civilized life, and embrace a faith that we could make a difference.

---

3. "About the Sustainable Development Goals," United Nations, *https://www.un.org/ sustainabledevelopment/sustainable-development-goals/*.

Author J.M. Coetzee has one of his characters say, "Faith means believing in what you do even when it does not bear visible fruit."[4] It takes an enormous amount of faith and hope to believe that one's own efforts will make a difference, sooner or later, on the larger page on which societies are written.

At BFW, young people competed for $9,000-a-year internships with health care. A staff member reluctantly gave up his car when the odometer reached 250,000 and the dials stopped registering. In 1989 someone donated a microwave, but many did not know how to use it because they could not afford one at home. As it turned out, it did not matter because the microwave blew the electrical circuits and had to be unplugged.

On the many nights we worked late, it was scary to walk the dark and isolated path to the Metro. There once was a shootout in the parking lot; another time, someone pulled the copper loose from the air conditioning unit on the roof; and yet another time, a guy stole boxes of hunger reports from one of our cars. When a staff member shouted from the third-floor window, "What are you doing down there?" the thief shouted back, "Stealing your stuff." Bemused by his honesty, we wondered what the street value of a hunger report might be. Since then, BFW has upscaled salaries and offices.

We shared a sense of solidarity, values, and vision, because we were working together to help people who were poor and hungry. It was an exhausting day-to-day slog that did not often feel spiritual. But our goal was not to have "spiritual experiences." The spirituality came from working for justice (political spirituality) in solidarity with and for others (social spirituality)—a spirituality that strengthened and celebrated our relational, social, moral, and political existence by doing things that helped people who experienced profound suffering and sometimes death.

It was spiritual in many senses: a commitment to values and vision that affirmed goodness; participation that worked to realize those

---

4. J.M. Coetzee, *The Childhood of Jesus* (London: Random House, Vintage Books, 2013), 35.

values; solidarity relationships in working with others; and results that improved the human spirit in the real world. If you tracked down those former staff today, you would find that for most, it was not a starter job but part of a lifelong commitment. A spiritual calling. The first three years at BFW, I was a grassroots organizer, traveling to meet members and prospects—to preach, teach, and lead workshops in churches and college campuses in eight states.

To save money, flights often required two or three stops. Organizers stayed overnight with regular dues-paying activists instead of in hotels because it was more economical and helped us understand and bond with members. On a tight budget, it was worth driving an extra hour for Denny's five-dollar spaghetti, salad, and roll. Another day, another Denny's. That was fine with me because, as the child of Depression-era parents, the definition of "good food" was cheap heaps of eats.

We had salaries, however modest, whereas local members were paying dues and contributing time on top of their regular jobs, children's dance lessons, soccer practice, and congregational and community activities. The members were awesomely inspiring, not only for their political work with Bread for the World, but because of their moral commitment and the values they evidenced in other parts of their lives, such as volunteering at food banks, soup kitchens, Meals on Wheels, and congregational suppers. They lived a committed spirituality of "family + congregation + charity + citizenship," a.k.a. charitable politics.

I met Vivian, who with her husband, made jelly, raised their children, milked their goats, convened a local group of people to learn about legislation and write letters to Congress, convinced the very conservative newspaper editor of her northwest city to include an article that supported funding for the Special Supplemental Nutrition Program for Women, Infants, and Children (WIC), met with her member of Congress when he was in town, and flew cross-country to visit him in his Washington office.

Many BFW members were involved in local and state as well as national politics. One morning in Louisiana, as I descended the wrought iron staircase from the guest room, I saw a relative of the host who had shown up unexpectedly seeking a place to sleep after I had gone to bed. There, sprawled face-down on the sofa bed in his tighty-whities, was a member of the Louisiana legislature. I ate breakfast and left without seeing his face. Probably just as well.

Many BFW members were steeped in policy choices, while others had a general idea of relevant policies and trusted that BFW was pursuing the best paths. On another trip I stopped for dinner with retired missionaries who had expressed interest in BFW. Grant Wood could have painted them as "American Gothic in the Northwest." She served a family-style chicken dinner. Her husband was silent, so she and I attempted polite conversation about my children and their grandchildren. A model airplane hung by a white string directly over his head. After a while, he stood up without saying a word, wound the propeller, and sat back down. The plane circled above his head. I thought, "OK, his mind is gone."

Then he broke the silence to say the plane hung there to entertain their grandchildren and he thought I might enjoy it. He then launched into a barrage of questions about the effects of the World Bank's structural adjustment policies. Not just the policies in general. Not just how they affect Africa. But the specific effects on the country in Africa where they had served. He had been waiting for us to get over the small talk. His questions circled over my head while the plane rotated over his. She said she wanted to come to DC to lobby the World Bank to change structural adjustment policies.

There is a huge amount of trust among communities of the politically committed. While organizing for BFW, I stayed with physicians who put me up for the night but left early and trusted me to lock the house when I left. After I ate the breakfast laid out on the kitchen table, I was touched to see their wedding vows handwritten, framed, and hung on the living room wall.

I once had a noon meeting in Shreveport, Louisiana, an evening meeting in Ruston, and planned to go on to Monroe for the night.

I phoned the host to warn that I would not arrive until nearly midnight. She said that she would leave the driveway light on. At 11:30 p.m. I pulled into what I hoped was the correct driveway. I hoisted a bag in each hand and trudged to the door. Hazel, surely in her eighties, asked if I was hungry and showed me upstairs to a bedroom. A small box of chocolates was on the nightstand. Fresh flowers were in a vase.

Though she lived alone, she welcomed a total stranger into her home late at night without question. She trusted that someone from BFW was safe. Whatever Miss Hazel prepared, I ate, cholesterol be damned. Breakfast was eggs, sausages, grits, and a large helping of U.S. assistance policies toward Africa. She said her grandson worked on Capitol Hill.

A decade later, I told the Miss Hazel story to the board of the Canadian Foodgrains Bank. During the break, a board member said that Hazel was his aunt, that she had died, that his kids had loved going to Louisiana to spend time with her, and that she always treated other people as she treated me. An invisible, spiritual thread connects those who work for personal and social kindness: for justice.

I also worked with Jim and Rebecca in Houston who, in addition to their local social service activities, mobilize locals and write letters to the editor and opinion editorials to influence readers and Congress. And there are hundreds more, each in their own way, yet all together in anonymous solidarity, working to help people disappearing into the dark holes of human desperation.

The members of Bread for the World are among the heroes of democracy—citizen saints of American society. Day after day, they sacrificially persevere on behalf of a vision of healthy families and societies. They organize and educate people on pending legislation and how to influence outcomes through strategic and timely processes— study and action groups, emails, letters, phoning and visiting legislators, writing opinion editorials in the local newspaper. They spark the warming fires that build and sustain democracies. They do it quietly, with determination and persistence as a spiritual discipline.

Grassroots organizing was morally and spiritually uplifting. Teaching seminary students had been enjoyable, though most of the faculty believed that courses on Bible, history, and theology were much more important than support for poor people, people of color, women, LGBTQ+, and were threatened by an emphasis on conscientization and advocacy. Fortunately, attitudes have shifted since then.

Being an organizer at BFW was not the most prestigious or best paid job I ever had. The travel was exhausting, and I got tired repeating the same message three times a day, day after day. There were the typical gripes, grievances, jealousies, and administrative dysfunctions. Nevertheless, staff, members, collegial agencies, members of Congress, and like-minded people in other countries around the world carried the fire together no matter how inconvenient, tiring, and difficult it sometimes became, because we were making a moral difference with our lives in the real world by helping those who needed it most.

Family and civic engagement in the context of a community of those who share these values is an important part of the meaning of life, and the possibility of—the hope for—the future. If there are any spiritual works in the world, they are these socially and politically productive spiritual callings. If, as many say, "God is good," then these are the works of the people of God, whether or not they use the word "God," though most staff and members of Bread for the World did, since BFW courted a religious constituency.

The Fire Kisses My Soul

The civil rights movement of the 1960s had originally lit a pilot light in my soul, though family, church, schools, and the Boy Scouts had laid the groundwork. Sometimes I say that the civil rights movement saved my soul. The movement sparked awareness of societal deformations and corruptions and suggested there were things I could do to make a difference. The movement seared my soul with a kiss.

A school classmate sent a faded photo of our 1940s Cub Scout Den in blackface. We didn't know any better. High school photos capture me proud—black tailcoat tux, wing collar, and bow tie—the White Mr. Interlocuter in a 1950s minstrel show. ("Rastus. Who was that lady I saw you with last night?") The civil rights movement sparked the embers of nascent values into a fire that started the long process of burning away cultural ignorance and rot, but also a warmth that kept heart and hope alive.

Over the years, the varied movements for the protection of families, rights, and dignity have challenged countless individuals to pick up, carry, and share the values of civilized life, though cultural pressures to take the easy road continuously seduce. It helps to be part of groups who work to achieve high social values, because other people reinforce our identity and help us fight back our own worst impulses.

I started out professionally as a pastor "doing church," then discovered racial injustice and a glimmering notion that "doing politics" was also an important way to promote goodness. Most of the early years as a student, pastor, and professor were consumed by eighty-hour weeks of study, professional practice, and social activism, but as I became more attentive to "doing family," I became increasingly aware that caring for family was a profound source of spirituality in my life.

No wonder religions draw on family images—the Greek and Roman gods, God the father/mother/son/virgin daughter, the ancestors. Religions are predicated on natural and social relationships. When we nurture families, we expand social goodness and sustainability, and we enlarge the human spirit. Lives are saved—literally saved—from devastation. The planet is conserved. Society is strengthened. Civilized life edges forward. Not just another day trying to escape what James Wood of the *New Yorker* called "life as death-in-waiting."

Ralph Waldo Emerson said, "The purpose of life is not to be happy. It is to be useful, to be honorable, to be compassionate, to have it make some difference that you have lived and lived well." When asked to comment on "what it means to be human and what makes life worth living," environmental activist Bill McKibben responded,

"For me, questions about being human come down to questions about human solidarity. Another name for solidarity is love."[5] Helping carry the fire of human solidarity is a spiritual calling.

O Beautiful for Spacious Skies

Throughout history, people have had spiritual experiences and identified spiritual realities—forces lively, powerful, and larger than our individual existence—in sacred waters, rocks, hilltops, storms, eclipses, holy places, gods, people, and events; sometimes personal and sometimes not; sometimes creative and benevolent, sometimes destructive and punishing. Good spirits connected people with one another as well as with nature, blessing harvests, fertility, and rituals of social life, while evil spirits brought drought, illness, and death. These spiritual experiences were celebrated and preserved in scriptures, the arts, rituals, belief systems, moral codes, religious institutions, and they sometimes led to profound acts of self-sacrifice on behalf of other people.

We experience awe and wonder at nature's vitality, complex magnificence, and power. Spending time in nature has physical benefits such as a healthier immune system and lowered blood pressure. Nature spirituality has a significant place in the so-called environmental movement—so-called because the movement is really a preserve-for-us movement. If we disappeared, the rest of nature would eventually truck along doing what the rest of nature naturally does.

The year I turned sixty, my wife Carole and I climbed Mt. Kilimanjaro with professionals from the World Bank and staff from public health agencies who were attending the World Federation of Public Health Agencies, where Carole was the press agent. Nearing the top, we paused and looked up. Billions of fiery stars mysteriously sparkled overhead in the absence of the normal lights of civilization. It was the same sky our grandmothers saw from the fields of their farms. "For

---

5. David Heim, "The End of Being Human," an interview with Bill McKibben in *Christian Century*, July 3, 2019, 30–33.

my part, I know nothing with any certainty, but the sight of the stars makes me dream," said Vincent van Gogh, who knew something about starry nights. It was awesomely spiritual.

At the top of Kilimanjaro, a photographer took pictures of us holding signs about HIV/AIDS, malaria, and maternal health, and the images were published in news media throughout Africa. The climb, the stars, the top were a spiritual experience, but so are people.

At an earlier time and place, Matilda Olkin, a Lithuanian girl, celebrated nature in her diary:

> But the sun shines most
> In the eyes of the little girl
> Her eyes are bright, full of light.
> They greet her joyful world.
> A world bursting to life and filled with sunshine.
> "Good morning! Good morning!"

Not long thereafter, her family was taken into a field. Townspeople heard screams for an unbearably long time, then shots. Matilda, her family, and others were shot in the back because it was 1941 and they were Jewish.[6] Nature gave her life, but did not, could not, protect her because, though we celebrate nature, we also romanticize it.

Nature Doesn't Give a Damn

When nature's hurricane hit in 2012, George and Patricia Dresch were in their house at Sandy Hook along with their thirteen-year-old daughter. Patricia survived, but George and their daughter were swept out to sea. Fifty-one-year-old John Filipowiz and his son John Jr. were found "in each other's arms" in the basement of their house.[7] Nature gave life and took it away without caring who, how, or when. John and his son cared until nature took away their ability to care.

---

6. Matthew Shaer, "Finding Her Voice," *Smithsonian*, November 2018, 70–79.

7. Ian Frazier, "The Toll," *New Yorker*, February 11/February 18, 2013, 38–44.

Patricia Dresch cared. We care too. Caring for one another is what we do as humans. Sunsets, grey whales, and guinea hens can inspire but not console, motivate but not guide. We look to people for that. Nature exhibits huge vitality and power, but no moral passion. The wonders of nature may inspire us to moral acts that preserve nature, but nature itself is morally numb. Joyce Carol Oates muses in *A Widow's Story*: ". . . in nature there is no 'good,' no 'evil.' Only life warring against life."

Michael Crichton, best known for *Jurassic Park*, writes of nature: "Along with its beauty, you may also come to experience its fecundity, its wastefulness, aggressiveness, ruthlessness, parasitism, and its violence." A character in the novel elaborates, "Nature is fundamentally indifferent. It's unforgiving, uninterested. If you live or die, succeed or fail, feel pleasure or pain, it doesn't care."[8] Viruses that cause pandemics are as much a part of nature as butterflies, roses, and panda bears.

Due to our carelessness, we are rapidly reaching a turning point where Planet Earth may "decide" that we humans have overstayed our welcome. Nature will not prevent human-caused climate change just because we have reached a deeper level of personal mindfulness.

I use "nature" here partly as a proxy, a stand-in, for the many private spiritualities that can be helpful but tend to ignore important life-and-death realities. Personal spiritualities too easily become ends in themselves, me-spiritualities, rather than acts that increase the human spirit by saving lives, improving society, and sustaining nature.

"I Am Somebody, Black and Proud"

In 1965, I matriculated at the University of Chicago Divinity School to take a PhD in Ethics and Society. Episcopal priest Professor Gibson Winter had written *The Suburban Captivity of the Churches* and helped establish the Urban Training Center, famous for its urban plunge— clergy and nuns set loose in downtown Chicago in old clothes and with a few dollars briefly to experience the life of an urban outcast.

---

8. Michael Crichton and Richard Preston, *Micro* (New York: HarperCollins, 2011), xii, 126.

Professor Al Pitcher, ordained in the Congregational Church, served as a coordinating director of Martin Luther King Jr.'s marches in Chicago and as an advisor to Jesse Jackson's Operation Breadbasket. Professor Martin Marty and other faculty participated in civil rights marches in the South.

The Ethics field encouraged dissertations that engaged with the problems experienced by real communities attempting to find solutions to poverty, racism, discrimination. The University fed my mind; the community fed both heart and mind. It was a time when I knew for sure that I was alive, that life had meaning, direction, purpose, because I was involved in something bigger than, more than, myself; a time that fed and fired up the spirit of many.

Professor Pitcher suggested that my dissertation be a history of Operation Breadbasket, so I began going through files, participating in demonstrations, attending meetings, and nervously having breakfast at a new Black Muslim restaurant. Elijah Muhammed, who lived a few blocks away, had said we were "White devils."

As I ascended the steep stairs of a Southside Chicago building on Saturday morning to attend Breadbasket meetings, I heard a band, rocking with joyful religious fervor, a religious liturgy in support of justice politics with its own ritual language: "Black is Beautiful," "Black Power." Jesse stood on the school stage before his mostly Black political congregation and shouted, "I am somebody," and the crowd thundered, "I am somebody."

I am
    I am
Somebody
    Somebody
I am Black
    I am Black
And I am proud
    And I am proud

Verse and response, again and again, the sound roared off the walls and rolled down the stairs. The style was religious, the methods political, and the goal minority empowerment—personal, social, economic, political, and authentically spiritual because it articulated the best of the human spirit.

The thrumming spiritual energy of the meeting was carried in the cadence of gospel preaching, the rhythms of movement music, drums, and throbbing bass lines in evangelical call and response, and it energized the feeling that here was a diverse group of people working together to achieve one of the highest moral goals in American, indeed, world history. We were part of a tremendous movement rising to claim . . . no, to demand justice because we as individuals and as a nation had made so many immoral choices. We could see, feel, smell, and participate in carrying the fire.

When Martin Luther King Jr. was assassinated, Professor Pitcher said that it was not a good time for a White guy to be doing the history of a predominantly Black organization, so I switched to community participation in urban policy. But here, too, I witnessed people of diverse backgrounds investing hours and hours of their valuable time and energy working for the benefit of people in Uptown and Woodlawn.

Video footage of my first meeting in Uptown shows the youthful Bobby Rush, cofounder of the Illinois Black Panthers, helping locals organize.[9] In ensuing years, Rush went from outside to inside the system, becoming a member of the U.S. House of Representatives in 2000, the only person who ever defeated Barack Obama in an election.

During the 1968 Democratic Convention, I saw protesters surging through Grant Park as the police swung batons and sprayed tear gas. A few demonstrators taunted the National Guard: "Shoot me. Go ahead. Shoot to kill." The police decided that the marchers should not

---

9. The *American Revolution 2* (Chicago: Facets Multi-Media, 2002) DVD shows footage from that meeting and demonstrations at the 1968 Democratic Convention. But be forewarned that there is also an *American Revolution 2.0*, which is about militia groups.

go farther south on Michigan Avenue than the Convention Center at 18th Street because they feared increased violence beyond that point.

Comedian Dick Gregory, who lived in Hyde Park, reportedly shouted through a megaphone that he was inviting everyone to his house down our street. He said that if anyone asked why they were going beyond 18th Street, to tell them that they were on the way as a private citizen to his house.

Anyone who doubts the power of political participation to arouse deep spiritual commitments that lead to spiritual experiences has neither personally experienced or empathetically witnessed events such as occurred in the suffragist, labor, civil rights, feminist, LGBTQ+, and peace movements, as well as Tiananmen Square, Poland's Solidarity Movement, Hong Kong, Black Lives Matter, and the other social, economic, and political movements around the world.

The deep feeling of meaning comes from the sense that we are connected with something bigger than ourselves, with movements that are huge and historic; that we are part of a grand moral struggle; that we are using whatever abilities, power, and resources we have to help bend the long arc of the moral universe toward justice; that power, so often yoked to evil, is here yoked to good; and that we are doing our humble part to carry that fire.

As you read these words, someone is being permanently damaged by malnutrition, racism continues to damage lives, someone is unable to afford school or is shut out because of discrimination, someone is dying of a preventable disease, someone is being bought and sold while another is raped, refugees are drowning in their attempt to find a decent life, billions of anti-ecological acts are being committed. Many someones also need to be "fired up, ready to go."

Embodied Spirituality

Bob Miller, my research partner in graduate school, used to go on endlessly about how a proposed urban plan had such a different *meaning* for city planners than it had for local residents. He did not just say "meaning," like you might say "chair"; his voice would rise and fall passionately, the "MMEEEANNINGG" of the plan. I nagged him to define "MMEEANNINGG." He finally shot back with a friendly grin, "If you ask me that one more time, I'll punch you in the nose."[10]

I got his meaning and quit asking. Underneath, there was another message: some things are hard to define. "Meaning" and "spirituality" are such words. The popular conception seems to be that meaningful spiritual experiences create feel-good emotions that have elusive qualities that defy clear description, like awe, love, and hope. We sense them. We feel them. Then we try to figure out what they mean.

We know what a fork or a Fuji apple is, but there is no universally shared understanding of what spirituality is. Yet, many people across time have had meaningful spiritual experiences, however specific or vague. We often think of people who are spiritual as devout and pious, as distinguished from someone who focuses on secular, worldly, or everyday realities. Some spiritually inclined people think of spirituality as part of their higher self: "the spirit is willing, but the flesh is weak."

The spiritual is often seen as opposite to the material or physical, our spirits as superior to our bodies. It is a wretched juxtaposition since it is hard to have spiritual experiences if you don't have a physical body. "All flesh is grass, and all its beauty is like the flower of the field. The grass withers, the flower fades." Well, yes, but I am very fond of my flesh, well-aged and marbled though it is, and would miss it very much.

This is not a trivial point. Flesh counts. My flesh. Your flesh. Their flesh. When the flesh suffers, we suffer. When it is gone, it is really gone, and any experiences after death will be qualitatively different when "I ain't got no body."

---

10. Bob went on to become an effective and beloved member of the faculty at Baker University, Baldwin City, Kansas. Baker is the oldest continually operating university in Kansas.

The experiences we talk of as spiritual are rooted in our bodies and social lives as well as our minds and emotions, rooted in actions as well as feelings. Classical spiritualities recognized the place of sociality, power, morality, and the physical, objective aspects of spirituality. The gods were believed to bring tangible results—deliverance or destruction, crops or drought, wars and alliances.

The spirituality of *We Carry the Fire* is an embodied spirituality: gritty, often inconvenient, and difficult; always social, moral, and powerful. Social and political spirituality is not only a certain quality or flavor of experience, but the companion of doing something (spiritual work) that attempts to bring tangible results—the human spirit is diminished or grows, civilization moves backward or forward by dribs and drabs.

People speak of spiritual awakenings: Paul on the road to Damascus, Martin Luther in a thunderstorm, Joan of Arc's visions, mystics of many faiths, spiritual gurus who will help you find the path to your own personal enlightenment. Religious revivals are often called awakenings. Many of those who experience such awakenings rise to lives of profound service on behalf of others, while many others' spiritual experiences are nothing more than sentimental piety.[11]

Serious awareness of desperate poverty, slavery, preventable death, cruelty, the possibility of massive destruction of human, plant, and animal life is also an awakening—an awakening to the degradation of the human spirit and the rest of nature, an awakening to the possibility of making a difference.

Let me say it again, because the spirituality we are talking about here is so different than what we often think of when we hear the word "spirituality." The goal of social and political spirituality is to help life become better for one another personally and politically, to act in the most intimate and the largest possible contexts to express love—something considerably different than the search for a "woo-woo" feeling.

---

11. My *Up from Apathy* (Nashville: Abingdon Press, 1983) documents interviews with eighty-seven people about the experiences that led them to become morally aware and socially involved.

The Seven Ms of Spirituality

Historian of Religion Amanda Porterfield says, "Spirituality refers to personal attitudes toward life, attitudes that engage an individual's deepest feelings and most fundamental beliefs."[12] Philosopher Richard Rorty describes spirituality as "the hope for a world in which human beings live far happier lives than they live at the present time."[13] Theologian David Ray Griffin describes spirituality as the "ultimate values and meanings [that] reflect some presupposition as to what is *holy*, that is, of ultimate importance" regardless of content, even "something very worldly, such as power, sexual energy, or success."[14] The Dali Lama suggests that spirituality is "the full blossoming of human values that is essential for the good of all."[15]

The strong adjectives they use—deepest, fundamental, ultimate, full blossoming, far happier, holy—suggest the depth, and the nouns—attitudes, feelings, beliefs, and values—suggest loci of spirituality.

The great classical spiritualities, the traditions I am calling on for insight, include at least seven characteristics. For mnemonic purposes, I offer the *Seven Ms of Family and Citizenship as Spiritual Calling*, or, more simply, *Social and Political Spirituality*:

> *Mystery*—something difficult to understand, indefinable, beyond perceptible reality and rationality.
>
> *More-Than*—not just more of something, but also a desire for more, for wider and deeper experiences, accomplishments, or connections, secular or religious, moral or immoral.

---

12. Gail Graham Yates, "Spirituality and the American Feminist Experience," *Signs*, Autumn 1983, 60, quoting Amanda Porterfield, *Feminine Spirituality in America—From Sarah Edwards to Martha Graham* (Philadelphia: Temple University Press, 1980), 59–72.

13. Richard Rorty, *An Ethics for Today* (New York: Columbia University Press, 2011), 14.

14. David Ray Griffin, "Introduction: Postmodern Spirituality and Society," in Griffin, ed., *Spirituality and Society* (Albany: State University of New York, 1988), 1.

15. Jeffrey Paine, "Religion Review: The forging of a holy man," *Washington Post*, January 23, 2011, B7, quoting the Dalai Lama, *My Spiritual Journey* (New York: HarperOne, 2009).

Moral—goodness or rightness of human virtue, intentions, actions, and results.

Mighty/Muscular—power, the ability to act.

Meaningful—sense of significance.

Methods—structured practices and spiritual disciplines.

Memories—institutionalized myths and lists that cull, carry, and shape individual and collective identity over time.

All spiritualities include a sense of *mystery* and *meaning*, a desire for a connection with something *more-than* (nature, the universe, God, a Messiah, ancestors), accompanied by positive feelings toward oneself and others, though many popular ones seem mostly to be "all about me." Many popular spiritualities minimize *morality* and *muscularity/power* or limit power to self-actualization. Even when *muscularity/power* is expressed toward society, it is seen as a possible byproduct rather than a constitutive element of a fully actualized spirituality.

"Doing good after the retreat" should not be an add-on—something that might or might not happen; it should be where we begin—action spirituality. Not just thinking or feeling, but doing. Twenty-five million Russians died in World War II, no matter how hard they prayed, how much they loved their families, or how many spiritual retreats they attended. What if we had been able to prevent that war?

Doing grassroots organizing at Bread for the World had a social and political spirituality of solidarity on behalf of a greater (*more-than, moral, mighty, meaningful*) cause with distinctive educational and political strategies (*methods*), and *memories* of others who came before us and were *mysteriously* working with us around the globe toward similar ends.

This deeper spirituality recognizes our bonds with other people and the highest values of the human spirit through history, something more than consumer spirituality in an entertainment-driven society. There are spiritual results. More people go to school. Fewer die of malnutrition. People have incomes, health care, and the ability to nurture others. Pollution declines. The climate is stabilized. The nukes are not used, and digital networks are mostly used for constructive purposes.

"the meaning of life": More Than 42

Lowercased, "the meaning of life" suggests something both smaller and yet larger than "the meaning of life and the universe," which in Doug Adams's *The Hitchhikers Guide to the Galaxy* is 42. When supercomputer Deep Thought is asked the meaning of life, it thinks for seven and a half million years and finally answers 42, though unfortunately, by then it can no longer remember what the question was. Monty Python's answer when asked about meaning of life was: "people are not wearing enough hats," which makes about as much sense as most answers we read.

When I told my students that the final class would include a segment on the meaning of life, some snickered while others laughed out loud. But I said, people find meaning in all sorts of pursuits—love, stamp collecting, jobs, clubs, triathlons, nature walks, sports, riches, pets, sex, social status, fashion. We buy T-shirts with the names of our favorite players. When our team wins, we somehow feel that we have won something, that we are part of something larger, something *more-than* that counts.

For some people, meaning begins with the opportunity to eat, the chance to go to school, freedom from oppression. The person who is starving experiences food as so satisfying that this experience participates in a fundamental, physical surplus or exuberance of meaning—their blood continues to pump, their eyes see, their voices are heard, survival, health. Gandhi said, "There are people in the world so hungry, that God cannot appear to them except in the form of bread." Exerting the *muscle* needed to bring *meaning* to others as well as ourselves is essential to the spiritual calling to carry the fire.

Chapters 3 and 4 on political spirituality are presented first because political spirituality is less often seen as a core element in spirituality. Most people have actively participated in some sort of "family" or sharing community (chapters 5 and 6). Chapters 7 and 8 argue that religious congregations for all their limitations and faults are an expression of our nature as social beings and provide spirituality with benefits. Chapter 9 helps us get from here to there, to our spiritual calling.

"Those Who Give Light"

Those who give light
must endure burning,
for the whole world will gather
to see this bright thing,
their burning
alive in the thick darkness and numbing cold
of the world's wintry waning.

Sun, moon, and stars illumine the way,
but the worldly wise seek direction
from one another
so that they may hold their palms
to the warmth of this new thing,
to see their own shadowy images
dancing on the walls while flickering yellowish music
provides accompaniment.

With a multitude of camels and cameras,
accretions of accommodations, accoutrements,
and musical adaptations, they will crown,
hallow, and sanctify,
examine, explain, expedite, and extol.
They will give gold, frankincense, and
sermons—

Useless gifts to one who burns for justice,
whose fire ignites to melt crowns
not to wear them,
to inflame the poor, crush the oppressor,
burn down institutions that cast shadows
and block the deliverance of the light
of the world.

Yet some will come to the light in kinship,
rekindling themselves to endure, and
Renewed and refreshed by the one
whose flame burns behind the shadows,
will travel home by another way recalling
how their hearts burn within them
to give light.

—*Jim Benton, 2015*

CHAPTER 2

The Kindling and the Sparks

All these things he saw and did not see.

—*The Road*

Gobbling Nothingness

The desire for more is hardwired in us and an important factor in our evolutionary progress. We desire to achieve more, experience more, create more, live longer. We seek more knowledge, possessions, success, justice, wealth, love, food, inventions, discoveries, points in games, speed, drugs, worlds. We desire to connect our lives with larger structures of meaning—God, country, famous people, political parties, sports teams—than our tiny, fragile, limited selves.

Yet, we are constrained by intrinsic physical and mental capacities. We literally cannot touch the stars or even the building across the street from where we sit. Our bodies cannot simultaneously be past, present, and future. Philosopher Martha Nussbaum suggests that "Human limits structure the human excellences and give excellent action its significance."[1] We find meaning in transcending normal limitations.

The search to connect our lives with more-than, greater-than, better-than, is one of the most powerful human drives and a root of both positive and negative spiritual experiences: the Olympics and Mount Olympus, saints and sinners, heroines and heroes both real and mythological. A deeply embedded quest for more-than is a spiritual quest, a soul quest that rises from the very center of our being. Most of us are committed to many "gods" that provide a sense of

---

1. Martha C. Nussbaum, *Love's Knowledge* (New York: Oxford University Press, 1990), 378.

meaning—from family to jobs, from race to country, from God to the good life however defined.

If we are going to seek more of something, it matters what that something is. Novelist Neil Gaiman describes, "new gods growing in America . . . gods of credit card and freeway, of Internet and telephone, of radio and hospital and television, gods of plastic and of beeper and of neon. Proud gods, fat and foolish creatures, puffed up with their own newness and importance" that distract us from humane values.[2] Distraction, greed, consumerism, self-indulgence justified by the banner of personal freedom without a balancing ethos of responsibility and commitment to the common good—how about deciding to seek less stuff and more goodness?

Polls, advertising, and spending patterns provide insight into cultural values, desires, and search for meaning—the spiritual gods of our lives. Ad and marketing agencies know us well, because tall buildings full of smart and creative people spend billions of dollars thinking about, designing, and pitching their products to us—some good for us, others useless or bad but good for someone's bottom line.

Ads transport us to Rome where we dine in the Piazza Navona, gazing at the Bernini Fountain while sharing a bottle of red wine with a romantic partner. Or a lounge outside a Swiss chalet, perhaps a massage at a private suite built over the water at the Bora Bora Hilton.

Clothing ads tell us their line is "classic," "suits your style," "impressive" because we want to feel important, "more individually me" because I have a $7,000 purse. The ads seduce at all ends of the economic spectrum. A local youth was killed for $700 sneakers because marketing convinced him and the thief that people will think they are cool dudes—not just another kid on the block—when they wear the shoes. Many of the desires that drive our inner spirit are culturally manufactured.

Carole and I were invited to look through the closets of a recently deceased woman of substantial means. She labeled her expensive garments with the date and place where she had last worn them, so not to

---

2. Neil Gaiman, *American Gods* (New York: Harper Torch, 2001), 137–38.

wear them there again. The gowns and furs hung in a ghostly house. The good experience died with the owner. Is that all there is in life? Is that what our lives, "as brief as the winking of a firefly," are called to? Is that the best way to help humanity's slow struggle to survive and thrive? Sure, she had pleasure picking them out and wearing them once or twice. But how many gowns, how many pairs of expensive shoes does anyone need to feel good about themselves, to prop up their ego, to feel more-than, better-than their peers? What were the social trade-offs for her moments of pleasure? Yes, jobs were created when her gowns and furs were produced and sold, but what quality of jobs, how much did the garment makers earn and under what conditions? What was the environmental cost?

The 3,000 factories in Xintang, China produce 800,000 pairs of jeans a day. It takes 700 gallons of water "to grow the cotton for one mass-produced T-shirt. . . . [U]p to 20 percent of mass-produced clothing does not sell . . . (but) is buried, shredded, burned, or carted out to landfills. . . . Fashion production consumes a stagger-ing 25 percent of all the chemicals made on earth and is responsible for nearly 20 percent of worldwide water pollution."[3]

We use up valuable resources, both natural and human, to create and purchase stuff instead of, say, improving schools and health care. We spend $10 billion on cosmetic surgery in the United States; in contrast, the annual per capita income of a billion people in the world is less than $500.[4] Plastic surgery can help people disfigured by birth, accident, illness, or assault. But most plastic surgery is a product of dis-torted cultural values.

IbisWorld says that Americans spend more than $2 billion on palmistry and related mystical services. We spend more than $100

---

3. Cintra Wilson, "Waste Not, Shop Not," *New York Review of Books*, February 27, 2020, 21–23, a review of Dana Thomas, *Fashionopolis: The Price of Fast Fashion—and the Future of Clothes* (New York: Penguin Press, 2019), https://www.nybooks.com/articles/2020/02/27/fast-fashion-waste-not-shop-not/.

4. Florence Williams, "Adam's Rib, van Gogh's Ear, Einstein's Brain," a review of Hugh Aldersey-Williams, *Anatomies: A Cultural History of the Human Body* (New York: W.W. Norton, 2013), *New York Times Book Review*, August 11, 2013, 14.

billion on fast food each year, more than fifty million meals a day for food that is typically not very good for our health or the environment. Those who carry the fire challenge the gods of our cultural ethos—the gods, both material and spiritual, that empty us out and pull us down, rather than fill us and lift us up.

In Ovid's *Metamorphoses*, the goddess Famine is commanded by Ceres to punish Erysichthon. Ceres departs quickly because her proximity to Famine leads her to begin to feel famished. Famine visits Erysichthon in his sleep, breathes into him. He dreams of great feasts.

> Chaws with his working mouth, but chaws in vain,
> And tires his grinding teeth with fruitless pain.

When he wakens, to get more food he sells all that he has, even his daughter, who the poet comments in an aside, "deserved a better father." Well, yes!

> At last all means, as all provisions, fail'd;
> For the disease by remedies prevail'd;
> His muscles with a furious bite he tore,
> Gorg'd his own tatter'd flesh, and gulph'd his gore.
> Wounds were his feast, his life to life a prey,
> Supporting Nature by its own decay.[5]

The story speaks to any unquenchable desire, a gut-deep craving that people try to fill with good things, bad things, sometimes making whatever sacrifices are required to get what they want. Desire is our soul's spiritual passion, our spiritual vocation for good and/or ill. "Consumerism is a religion that builds on the humanness of desire and promotes the impossible: satisfying all desires but harms both the poor and the affluent."[6] We need to re-educate our desires.

---

5. Ovid, "Impious Acts and Exemplary Lives," *Metamorphoses*, trans. Sir Samuel Garth, John Dryden, et al., *http://classics.mit.edu/Ovid/metam.8.eighth.html*.

6. L. Shannon Jung, "The Reeducation of Desire in a Consumer Culture," *Journal of the Society of Christian Ethics* (Spring/Summer 2012): 21–38.

In the Hebrew Scriptures, the prophet Haggai accuses the Israelites of being so caught up in their personal pursuit of more-than that they were neglecting to rebuild the temple. The critique seems primarily to have had a cultic motivation, but it's an interesting metaphor for what functions in many lives as a spiritual quest: souls yearning for more without taking into account which "more" is better than another.

. . . you eat, but you never have enough;

you drink, but you never have your fill;

you clothe yourselves, but no one is warm;

and you that earn wages earn wages

to put them into a bag with holes.

—Haggai 1:6

Haggai says they lead shallow, self-serving lives and ignore religious realities. They come and they go. They build and they buy. They work and they eat. But amid the busyness of daily life, they are oblivious to the depth of their existence, so they are never fully satisfied—"You eat, but you never have enough; you drink, but you never have your fill," pouring their lives, their souls, their center of being into a bag with holes.

Even we who work hard and try to live modest lives sometimes wonder how much we pour our lives, bit by bit, day by day, into a bag that leaks out the bottom almost as fast as we pour ourselves in at the top. We work but the results are frequently unsatisfying. We say we love our family but are too busy to spend meaningful time with them. We attend spiritual retreats, but by Wednesday the spark has dimmed so we schedule more retreats.

Self-help and spirituality books attempt to fill holes in our heart, but we still have trouble joining the great choir of humanity singing the Hallelujah Chorus, because to do that we would have to show up for choir practice and interact with other people in the chorus. We are more likely to stay home and listen to a recording of Leonard Cohen singing "Hallelujah"—beautiful, haunting, spiritual, but lonely.

Do we find the deep meaning and satisfaction that comes from connecting our lives with the most important *more-thans* in the world? Are we making a difference as individuals, and collectively as a society and nation? Are we helping create a healthful future for all, or just feeling needy or anxious about what lies ahead for ourselves? Are we helping civilization move forward or merely patching leaks in our individual lifeboats?

The teacher in Ecclesiastes says, "Vanity of vanities, all is vanity." He tries pleasure. He builds houses, creates gardens and vineyards, buys slaves, accumulates gold and silver. What do people gain from all their toil in the sun? he asks. "A generation comes, and a generation goes, but the earth remains forever." Those who carry the fire have a view of the long-haul good of humanity, not just immediate experiences and possessions.

Part of the problem is that our unreflective, asocial, value decisions get made piecemeal within the context of taken-for-granted normal daily practice, and we ignore the larger societal and environmental consequences that flow from them. This applies to virtually all our choices—what we wear, what we eat, how we travel. Religious congregations sometimes also contribute to negative practices. The "God wants you to be rich" prosperity gospel is obvious, but there are subtler ways, for example the Sunday brunch with unhealthy body- and planet-damaging food.

When I began teaching Church in Society at a divinity school, a social worker agreed to show me around so I could understand local realities and be better prepared to share local realities with students. Every pastor/priest/rabbi/imam/guru should be required to do this.

We visited a Hispanic home where five children milled around the living room. Both parents were at work. It was Monday, so we gently asked the children why they were not in school. A tiny girl responded, "We don't have shoes."

"All God's children have shoes," sings the African American spiritual, well, at least in heaven, if not here, the singers reassure one another. The problem is not shoes *per se*. It is proportionality, those who have too many shoes or spend too much on shoes, while others do not have any.

Sports, both amateur and professional, are an important and largely positive part of culture. But would we buy a ticket to a Denver Broncos game instead of purchasing the equivalent twenty-two mosquito nets to protect children from malaria? Sure, because we live inside cultural cocoons in which we make choices without thinking about the possible effect on those who have the bad luck to be born in different circumstances. I do it, you do it, we all do these sorts of things all the time.

Nicholas Kristof describes a woman who had lost a child to malaria and each night had to decide which of the seven remaining children and grandchildren got the only net to ward off malaria they might contract that night.[7] Tickets versus mosquito nets does not have to be a zero-sum game. The problem is not just buying this or that, but those parts of our cultural ethos that lead to distorted desires and distracted searches for more-than, unbalanced by deep awareness of the consequences that occur to other people, the environment, our own well-being and sense of meaning and responsibility.

What is it about our cultural priorities that we can't afford to end poverty, provide adequate health care, address climate change, but that we couldn't wait to get out of the house during COVID-19 to spend money being entertained in restaurants, movie theaters, shops, and sports?

It is not just a matter of middle-class guilt or beating ourselves up about all the good we could be doing, but do not. The one percent typically waste the most because they consume the most and therefore contribute more to environmental decline. Many people of substantial means also use their wealth to influence the political system primarily to benefit themselves. Steep inequality of income has led to steep political inequality. But remember, we with less money have more people to organize campaigns, and more votes. If, *IF* (big if) we focus more on the common good and less on disposable goods.

---

7. Nicholas D. Kristof, "A Way of Life Is Ending. Thank Goodness," *New York Times Sunday Review*, September 29, 2013, 13.

Soldiers who experience the traumas of war can suffer "moral injury." When we fail to address the suffering of others and the planet, we not only harm them, but slowly, day after day, we wound, damage, numb our souls, and commit soul injury.

Horatio Alger Had Lucky Bootstraps

The typical justification used for unneeded consumption by individuals and obscene incomes for those who are disproportionately rich is, "I deserve it" or "I earned it." Our lives and accomplishments, however, are a balance between luck and choice, in which luck plays, by far, the largest part. Senator Elizabeth Warren catches some of the moral implications when she says:

> There is nobody in this country who got rich on their own. Nobody! . . . You built a factory out there? Good for you. But . . . You moved your goods to market on roads the rest of us paid for. You hired workers the rest of us paid to educate. . . . God bless! Keep a big hunk of it. But part of the underlying social contract is you take a hunk of that and pay forward for the next kid who comes along."[8]

She is right, but the social reality is much deeper.

Martha Nussbaum quotes *Antigone*, which describes our precarious lives as a "life lived 'on the razor's edge of luck.'"[9] Nine innocent people drowned when beer vats burst in the great London beer flood of 1814, and twenty-one were killed when a tank of molasses burst in Boston in 1919.[10] People who worked in the Twin Towers on 9-11 lived because they took a cigarette break or missed their plane. Others died.

---

8. Sheelah Kolhatkar, "Rethinking Elizabeth Warren," *Bloomberg Businessweek*, September 16-22, 2013, *https://www.youtube.com/watch?v=AHFHznu-N-M*.

9. Martha C. Nussbaum, *The Fragility of Goodness: Luck and Ethics in Greek Tragedy and Philosophy*, second edition (Cambridge: Cambridge University Press, 2001), 89.

10. Michael Blastland and David Spiegelhalter, *The Norm Chronicles: Stories and Numbers about Danger* (London: Profile Books, 2013), 200.

Good luck and bad luck. Research suggests that the majority of cancer cases may be due to pure chance, the result of random cell mutations. Joan Ginther has won nearly $21 million in four jackpots. I knew a woman in California who won the lottery twice and yet died in her early thirties.

We might have been born of any race, and with our history of slavery and discrimination, race has made a huge difference. Slaves had no chance to build up the equity that White families began to accumulate during the same period of time. No chance to decide whether they could keep their family together.

Each of us could have been born into a household of any language or religion; of either gender or somewhere in between; in any century, nation, or circumstance to any family, or lack thereof. Someone was. You could have been that someone.

Suppose you had been born in Naka-ku, the central business district of Hiroshima on August 5, 1945. Your lifespan would have been one day. The atomic bomb fell on August 6. But Osamu Shimomura, who was nearby, thought the planes looked pretty. Though he was temporarily blinded by the flash, he eventually went on to be a Nobel Laureate in chemistry. You might have been one of the nearly 2,000 people killed in a mass shooting in the United States since 1966, most of them just because they were in the wrong place at the wrong time and because deranged shooters were not restrained.

The Horatio Alger rags-to-riches myth is deeply embedded in American culture. "It is a matter of individual responsibility to pull yourself up by your bootstraps." "Honesty and hard work pay off." "Keep your nose to the grindstone." (Ouch.) "It's your own fault if you fail," and by extension, "People who are rich deserve what they have, and people who are poor deserve to be poor because they are not willing to sacrifice and work hard."

Alger's books, such as *Luck and Pluck*, say it does take pluck—hard and often sacrificial work—to succeed. But Alger also shows that it also takes luck. His young hero does not have physical handicaps that prevent him from helping the woman in distress. It's luck that he's on that particular train at the right time, that he's on the spot where and when the woman is threatened by a thief, that the thief doesn't stab him, and that the woman is rich and beneficent. This does not negate or deny honesty, creativity, and hard work, but our cultural myth overlooks the role that good fortune and the beneficence of other people play in positive outcomes.

Randy Pausch was a professor of computer science at Carnegie Mellon University in Pittsburgh, Pennsylvania. A month before his forty-sixth birthday, he was diagnosed with pancreatic cancer, and months later he was told he had three to six months of good health left. Carnegie Mellon's departing professors could give a last public lecture. Randy's first on-stage comment was: "I won the parent lottery."[11]

Others say, "I belong to the lucky sperm club." We have the good, or bad, luck to be born in a certain family, a specific gender and color, with certain potential abilities and disabilities, in this or that nation and century. Change those variables in a major way, and everything—repeat, *everything*—changes for us.

Who should get credit for being born with an IQ of 160 rather than 60? Who chooses to be born able or with a severely disabling condition? Who should get credit for being born a child prodigy—a Mozart, Sor Juana Inés de la Cruz, or Blaise Pascal? Never discount the role that luck plays in our lives, especially at the beginning. There are no self-made wo/men. There are people born with certain gifts and possibilities who work hard and become more successful than the rest of us. But not without having received the gifts of birth and the contributions of other people.

An estimated "60 percent of a person's income is determined merely by where she was born (and an additional 20 percent is dictated by how rich her parents were)."[12] Those who claim they deserve

---

11. Randy Pausch with Jeffrey Zaslow, *The Last Lecture* (New York: Hyperion, 2008). The lecture is available on YouTube.

12. Catherine Rampell, "Thy Neighbor's Wealth," citing Branko Milanovic, *The Haves and the Have-Nots, New York Times Book Review*, January 30, 2011, 17.

what they have because they earned it, take too much credit. While they deserve credit for what they have done, they ignore the accident of their birth and the supportive human community that enabled them to succeed.

Life is not fair. It is our task to choose to make it fairer for those whose accident of biology, sociology, geography, gender, race, or other circumstance leave them on the bad side of luck. Ben S. Bernanke, former chair of the Federal Reserve, said in a Princeton commencement address that "people who are the luckiest . . . reap the largest rewards" and therefore "have the greatest responsibility . . . [to] contribute to the betterment of the world and to share their luck with others."[13]

Moral Grounding

A cruel sadist may have ecstatic, for him, "spiritual experiences," but the spirituality we seek is one that is grounded in morality. A more-than experience is not, by itself, sufficient any more than mystery by itself is sufficient for spirituality. Goodness/morality/ethics are defining characteristics of a transformative spiritual calling.

In everyday conversation, we use the word "good" in both moral and morally neutral ways to describe different kinds of experiences—the goodness of health and happiness, of laughter and lunch, of personal growth and helping others, of sciences and the arts. And all such experiences, when extraordinarily intense, have a spiritual dimension.

When it comes to moral decisions, philosophical and theological ethics can help us think through nuances of complex moral concepts and practices. It is, however, often impossible to translate general ethical insights and scriptural injunctions into specific decisions, actions, or public policies. "Love your neighbor" is a wonderful guide, but there is no clear path from there to the details of how health care should be funded.

---

13. "Commencement Speakers," *New York Times National*, June 16, 2013, 20.

Empirical studies can also help us sort out the truth or falsity of contesting claims and make better decisions. Facts do matter. Responsible participation in a democracy means that we take on the burden of becoming as informed as possible, but how many of us take time to dig up the necessary information? Even members of Congress may only be truly expert on the issues covered by the committees on which they serve.

The empirical facts of a given case are sometimes unclear, debatable, or unavailable. Take the Supplemental Nutrition Assistance Program (SNAP, formerly the Food Stamp Program) as example. Liberals emphasize the nutritional benefits to individuals and the community. Conservatives emphasize cost, corruption, and dependency.

Let's begin by asking what welfare is and why is it needed. From one point of view, welfare is a compensatory allocation from public funds for deficiencies in wages not paid by private companies, pressure by those who have the ear of legislators that keep public infrastructure, education, and health care underfunded, market decisions about who works and doesn't (closing a coal mine and leaving miners stranded), alongside bad decisions or the natural limitations of individuals.

Studies (before the pandemic) suggested that about 40 percent of recipients of SNAP are White, 28 percent are Black, 10 percent are Hispanic, 2 percent are Asian, and 1 percent are Native American. "Around 80 percent of SNAP benefit users either have children (40 percent), are disabled (20 percent), or are over the age of sixty-five (17 percent)" and not fully able to work, or find jobs that make them self-sufficient, despite claims that they are just lazy.[14]

Data suggest that many people just need help to get through a short-term crunch, such as losing a job or getting a divorce.[15] It's also true that some recipients become dependent or have figured out ways

---

14. Elizabeth W. Crew, "Who Really Received Food Stamps?" SWHelper, April 4, 2016, *https://www.socialworkhelper.com/2016/04/04/really-recieves-food-stamps/*.

15. Arthur Delaney, "How Long Do People Stay on Public Benefits?" HuffPost, May 29, 2015, *https://www.huffingtonpost.com/2015/05/29/public-benefits-safety-net_n_7470060.html*.

to scam the system, though not on the scale of those who are greedy in law, commerce, government, and sometimes even religion.

Not everything is measurable or worth measuring. How do you measure the direct impact a program has in contributing to dependency of a specific individual when complex families may be on more than one program and have varied long-term life situations? One child may be led to greater dependency, while another strives to avoid the opprobrium of "welfare" and becomes a millionaire who creates jobs and contributes millions to the arts. The results of public policies are multifaceted, and the cost of granular monitoring is sometimes higher than any misspent amounts.

For better and worse, most people decide that food stamps and other programs are good or bad by their overall experience, their frame of reference, their stereotypes, their social networks, their values. And what most people believe counts, because their beliefs can influence policies and programs over time.

Research suggests that most of our first-level responses, including our moral responses, rise out of emotions and a gradually accumulated web of beliefs. When people hear something that corresponds with that web, they are likely to embrace it. When they hear something that differs, they tend to reject it, sometimes doubling down, even though the presenter claims that the information is empirically verifiable, rational, or scientific. The source of this "confirmation bias" seems to be structural and to arise from our intrinsic sociality.

We tend to believe what others around us believe and to seek out others who reinforce our established beliefs. The tendency to live inside a socially contextual web of beliefs may have risen out of an evolutionary process in which survival was highly dependent on binding together in cohesive social units to overcome the many hazards people faced.[16]

While we should affirm the critical importance of moral theories and empirical studies, families, religious congregations, and

---

16. Elizabeth Kolbert, "That's What You Think: Why Reason and Evidence Won't Change Our Minds," *New Yorker*, February 27, 2017, 66–71.

schoolteachers inculcate basic values. Most people who have experienced good socialization, including some with limited mental ability, make good moral judgments every single day without studying ethical theories or empirical studies. Good socialization can shape the moral values that lead to habitual ways of making sound decisions without even having to think about what is right or wrong in every case.

Primary and secondary socialization, along with people's daily social and cultural experiences, are the most important shapers of moral sensibilities and the way people translate them into specific beliefs and practices. This is one of many reasons the well-being of families, and public policies that support families, is a spiritual calling. Families shape initial core values, frames of reference, and the capacity for empathy within which people interpret what they hear. Religious communities have also played a vital role in this socialization and reinforcement process.

When making a moral judgment about a public policy, as well as many personal decisions, we must lean toward the values—the general moral guidelines—most of us were taught as children. Practice the habit of love, or at least of being kind, to your neighbor. Listen to the people who suffer most. They know where they hurt and often know why. They may be less clear about the remedies, but their perspective is a necessary starting point. And, of course, continue to familiarize yourself with ethical guidelines and empirical results.

It is important to choose the moral issues close to our hearts, to keep our minds open, and to listen to the opposition. What seems right to us now may not seem so correct later. Or the decision we advocated may have unintended consequences that lead us to reevaluate that decision. Listen relentlessly.

It also helps to join, contribute to, and follow one or more groups that do the necessary analysis and research on the concerns close to your heart. They have staff to think through various issues and keep track of what is going on, and they can keep you informed about when and how to respond in a timely manner.

It is also good to listen to at least one person with whom we disagree strongly on social issues. Their opinions come from their

experiences, just as ours do. Since people come from different experiences, education, communities, and have different life situations,
we are inevitably bound to disagree about which course of action is
best. Democracy is necessary as a way of structuring conversations and
making decisions that affect the whole body politic.

Strengthening democracy is our most urgent calling as a citizen,
perhaps more important than achieving this or that policy or practice
that we think is best, because democracy gives everybody at least a
formal chance of expressing how they think we should live together. I
count. But so do you, no matter how different our beliefs.

Enlarging Goodness Is a Spiritual Calling

People often claim that God is good and that, therefore, one of the
more difficult theological problems is why does evil exist, especially if
God is also seen to be all-powerful. It seems to me that deeply destructive evil is always present in the world, so our chief problem is not to
explain the presence of evil but to explain the presence of good. Why
does goodness exist in an often hostile, potentially vicious and fatal
natural environment?

The power of human goodness manifests itself sometimes under
the harshest and most unlikely conditions. Children play games in
refugee camps, burned-out buildings, and during wars. Prison inmates
provide literacy classes, health care, and other sorts of support and
encouragement to fellow inmates. People may disagree ritually and
theologically, sometimes violently, about the existence and nature of
God or the content of the good, but virtually all promote some notion
or other of goodness.

As you read this, millions of people around the world are experiencing and contributing to a greater goodness that is complex, mysterious, and powerful. Mysterious because, how do we account for
its universality, its power, the feeling of joy it can elicit when we have
a good experience or when we do a good deed? Why do people do
good deeds again and again across generations and centuries, across

separated geographies, races, even warring clans, tribes, and religions? In a universe that is continuously destroying as well as creating, there is no apparent cosmic reason for moral goodness to exist. But it does, at least in human experience.

A sense of moral values is part of what it means to be human because morality rises out of the social nature of our existence, the need to express empathy, to find rules and practices that keep us from harming one another, to bring a measure of orderliness and opportunities in society. A conviction that there is a moral order, or at least moral influence, is at the core of religious faiths.

A.C. Bhaktivedanta Swami Prabhupada writes, "The Muslim may become a Christian, or the Christian may become a Hindu. Such changeable faith, therefore, is not religion. However, if one be Hindu, Muslim, or Christian, one is always a servant. So the particular faith is not the religion; but service is the religion."[17]

Some say they do not believe that we can contribute to a greater goodness in the world. We do not have the ability to help transcend history. There is so much horror, so much unmitigated evil, pain, and suffering in the world that sometimes it's hard to see the goodness and even harder to believe that each of us can do something to mitigate it. There are many days when I identify with that view.

But consider a parallel to Pascal's wager. Blaise Pascal argued that you can bet your life by living as though God either exists or does not exist. Within his theological frame of reference, if you bet that God does not exist, then you are likely to spend eternity in hell, whereas if you live as though God exists, even though it is often inconvenient, you might go to heaven. He asks: Which is the better bet? Which gives you better odds if you are right: to experience temporal inconvenience while believing that God exists or eternal punishment if God does not? It is a decision about how you choose to live your life in the face of uncertain verities.

---

17. A.C. Bhaktivedanta Swami Prabhupada, "Introduction," in *The Bhagavad Gita as It Is* (New York: Collier Books, 1968), 33.

Take hell out of the equation and substitute good for God and you get something like Yann Martel's *Life of Pi*. Pi Patel tells the story of how, after a shipwreck, he shared a rowboat with a wild tiger for 227 harrowing days before coming safely to land. Insurance adjustors, concerned about why the boat sank, refuse to believe his fantastic tiger story. Exasperated, Pi asks if what they want to hear an alternative, "dry, yeastless factuality."

He proceeds to tell an alternative story in which four people survive the shipwreck—the cook, his mother, a young sailor, and himself. No tiger. In this version, the cook secretly gorges on their sparse supply of food, kills the sailor for fish bait, eats some of his dried flesh, kills Pi's mother, and then is murdered by Pi. Pi turns to the insurance men and asks which story they prefer: the boy and a wild tiger in uneasy coexistence or a series of horrendous acts of murder and cannibalism?

The existential question comes down to, "What story do we choose around which to fashion our lives?" Which among competing biographical narratives do we use to inform our beliefs and actions? "By deciding who we really are, we are deciding which side of history we want to be on and what kind of community we want to be part of."[18] This is a spiritual decision.

Personally, I prefer to construct my life on the premise that the miracle of moral goodness (always interlaced with evil) is a continuous part of human expression, that moral goodness is foundational to religious experience and texts, and that I can help make moral goodness thrive. Some might call this faith.

In J.M. Coetzee's *The Childhood of Jesus*, the boy asks, "Why are we here . . . what are we here for?" Simón responds, "We have been given a chance to live and we have accepted that chance. It is a great thing, to live. It is the greatest thing of all."[19] Albert Einstein said,

---

18. Paul Rogat Loeb, *Soul of a Citizen: Living with Conviction in Challenging Times* (New York: St. Martin's Press, 2010), 345.

19. J.M. Coetzee, *The Childhood of Jesus* (London: Random House, Vintage Books, 2013), 21.

"There are only two ways to live your life. One is as though nothing is a miracle. The other is as though everything is a miracle"—in this case, the miracle of the existence of moral goodness and our ability to enlarge it. The struggle of the human spirit to find a morally better way is a spiritual struggle.

Billions of people daily make deep sacrifices. They care for loved ones who are terminally ill or have advanced dementia. Franciscans, Maryknoll sisters and brothers, Peace Corps workers, Doctors Without Borders, ICU nurses and aides, and many others have made caring their daily job. The groups are too many to name or number, but they include the many people who labor daily in nonprofits, government agencies, and the military on behalf of a better world—who seek to extend goodness for others, often at great personal cost. They carry the fire; enlarging the realm of goodness is a spiritual vocation.

> We hold these truths to be self-evident, that all men are created equal, that they are endowed by their Creator with certain unalienable Rights, that among these are Life, Liberty and the pursuit of Happiness. —That to secure these rights, Governments are instituted among Men (sic), deriving their just powers from the consent of the governed. . . .
>
> —U.S. Declaration of Independence

This is a revolutionary spark that helped kindle the flame of democracy in what became the United States. This is the democratic, political, collective fire from which our ideals have emerged. This is part of the fire we seek to carry. Beneath the soaring rhetoric and monumental figures are the hallowed but unheralded contributions of people like us who hear the beating heart of humanity and respond.

"They Called Me Theirs, but I Hold Them"

I first read Ralph Waldo Emerson's *Hamatreya* in college, but later forgot the title and author. For half a century I quizzed English professors to find out which Anglo-American poet had written a poem with an Earth Song, but no one could identify the source. I was asking the wrong people. Emerson is not known for his poetry.

Hamatreya is said to have been inspired by the *Vishnu Purana*, a traditional Vedantic mythology.

> Bulkeley, Hunt, Willard, Hosmer, Meriam, Flint,
> Possessed the land which rendered to their toil
> Hay, corn, roots, hemp, flax, apples, wool, and wood.
> Each of these landlords walked amidst his farm,
> Saying, "'Tis mine, my children's and my name's.
> How sweet the west wind sounds in my own trees!
> How graceful climb those shadows on my hill!
> I fancy these pure waters and the flags
> Know me, as does my dog: we sympathize;
> And, I affirm, my actions smack of the soil."
>
> Where are these men? Asleep beneath their grounds;
> And strangers, fond as they, their furrows plough.
> Earth laughs in flowers, to see her boastful boys
> Earth-proud, proud of the earth which is not theirs;
> Who steer the plough, but cannot steer their feet
> Clear of the grave.
> They added ridge to valley, brook to pond,
> And sighed for all that bounded their domain;
> "This suits me for a pasture; that's my park;
> We must have clay, lime, gravel, granite-ledge,
> And misty lowland, where to go for peat.
> The land is well,—lies fairly to the south.
> 'Tis good, when you have crossed the sea and back,
> To find the sitfast acres where you left them."

Ah! The hot owner sees not Death, who adds
Him to his land, a lump of mould the more.
Hear what the Earth say:—.

EARTH-SONG

"Mine and yours;
Mine, not yours.
Earth endures;
Stars abide—
Shine down in the old sea;
Old are the shores;
But where are old men?
I who have seen much,
Such have I never seen.

"The lawyer's deed
Ran sure,
In tail,
To them and to their heirs
Who shall succeed,
Without fail,
Forevermore.

"Here is the land,
Shaggy with wood,
With its old valley,
Mound and flood.
But the heritors?—
Fled like the flood's foam.
The lawyer and the laws,
And the kingdom,
Clean swept herefrom.

"They called me theirs,
Who so controlled me;
Yet every one
Wished to stay, and is gone,
How am I theirs,
If they cannot hold me,
But I hold them?"

When I heard the Earth-song
I was no longer brave;
My avarice cooled
Like lust in the chill of the grave.[20]

In many churches, people sing "We give Thee but Thine own . . . all that we have is Thine alone" as the offering is brought forward. Virtually everything we have is a gift—in theistic language "a gift from God"—on loan to us from the natural, economic, social, political, and cultural lives of previous and concurrent generations. The possessions we hold are temporary. The land we hold, will hold us. All that we have comes as a temporary gift. We get to use for a while but not to possess forever.

Hunger, poverty, radical inequality, and destruction of the environment are bad stewardship. We cannot afford to lose human lives, talents, and energies. We cannot afford a declination of the human spirit and the destruction of earth. We have received the fires of civilization and are called to share and carry those fires forward, to be stewards of all, in theistic language, God's children (including ourselves), and all God's good earth. A moral calling. A moral vocation that provides a profound, deeply spiritual sense of meaning.

20. https://www.poetryfoundation.org/poems/52341/hamatreya.

Hinges of History

Meaningful, more-than, moral moments can become celebratory marking points, symbols of change, in our lives—moments of life transitions with deep spiritual meaning. An addict works hard, transcends their past, and celebrates sobriety every anniversary thereafter. A criminal repents and works with children to reduce delinquency. A child from the projects or a cotton farm works their way up the ladder and becomes a talented and contributing poet or political leader. A middle-class person who has largely been insulated from extreme poverty has an encounter with dramatic human suffering that leads them to act on behalf of people who are less fortunate.

There are also those large historical more-than, moral, and meaningful moments that carry spiritual and symbolic meaning—such as the fall of the Berlin wall and the first landing on the moon—that become hinges of history changing perceptions and practical realities.

The late Rep. John Lewis described the Obama nomination at the Democratic convention as a spiritual event that could happen because of the many sacrifices made by earlier generations of people who risked their lives, and sometimes were killed, protesting for basic civil rights. The nomination and subsequent swearing-in resonated with Lewis's deeply held values and the community of those of all races who struggled and sacrificed for justice.

At the same time, judging by the vitriol that followed, the Obama presidency was more-than evil, so profound that it attained spiritual, mythical, demonic significance for others. Not long thereafter, there were Trump supporters and opponents who seemed to adopt attitudes on both sides of the spiritual equation.

When we experience the mystery of connections with partners, children, friends, and, for theists, God, we can feel a sense of more-than, of being connected with wider, transcendent structures of meaning. Actively helping to achieve a transformative morality brings a deep and profound sense of meaning for us, but more importantly helps bring goodness to the beneficiaries of our efforts. Even if that which we do does not provide warm fuzzy feelings at the time, it is still a spiritual calling because the human spirit is enriched. Exerting the muscle to bring life to others as well as ourselves is an essential fire-carrying spirituality.

We Are Called to Act

'Tis written: "In the beginning was the *Word*."
Here am I balked: who, now can help afford?
The *Word*?—impossible so high to rate it;
And otherwise must I translate it,
If by the Spirit I am truly taught.
Then thus: "In the Beginning was the *Thought*."
This first line let me weigh completely
Lest my impatient pen proceed too fleetly,
Is it the *Thought* which works, creates, indeed?
"In the beginning was the *Power*," I read.
Yet, as I write a warning is suggested,
That I the sense may not have fairly tested.
The Spirit aids me: now I see the light!
"In the beginning was the *Act*," I write.[21]

—*Goethe, Faust, Scene III*

The creation story in *Genesis* begins with an action, "Let there be light," the creation of light, a manifestation of fire, not with contemplation. We each have a unique set of abilities that combine with an unrepeatable set of experiences in a particular social and historical moment that make it possible for us to make distinctive contributions. We are tiny beings in the great stream of society and history, not long alive, not long remembered. We are not just called to have great experiences, whether spiritual or secular, but to contribute to the larger

---

21. Johann Wolfgang Von Goethe, *Faust*, trans. Bayard Taylor (New York: Random House, Modern Library, copyrighted 1870 by Bayard Taylor, 1898 and 1912 by Marie Hansen Taylor), 43.

whole. "Activism is my rent for living on the planet," wrote author Alice Walker.[22]

Florence Nightingale, appalled by the medical conditions she witnessed in the Crimean War, initiated the process of collecting data about the performance of hospitals and surgeons so that standards could be examined and raised. She understood her data gathering to be more than just good works, but a spiritual endeavor, a spiritual calling.[23]

Dr. Gretchen Berggren, a longtime medical missionary, said of Dr. Davida Coady, who tirelessly worked on four continents to help people in greatest need, "For some of us, like Davida, this is a spiritual calling."[24]

In Abraham Verghese's novel, *Cutting for Stone*, Matron presses Marion to choose the hardest profession he can imagine. He balks.

"Why must I do what is hardest?" . . .

"Because, Marion you are an instrument of God. Don't leave the instrument setting in its case, my son. Play! Leave no part of your instrument unexplored. Why settle for 'Three Blind Mice' when you can play the 'Gloria'?" . . .

"But, Matron, I can't dream of playing Bach, the 'Gloria' . . ."

"No, Marion, she said, her gaze soft, reaching out for me, her gnarled hands rough on my cheeks. "No, not Bach's 'Gloria.' Yours! Your 'Gloria' lives within you. The greatest sin is not finding it, ignoring what God made possible in you."[25]

We have many kinds of callings. A soldier who is called to kill a terrorist may also feel called to love her family and support Planned

---

22. "Alice Walker Quotes," Goodreads, *https://www.goodreads.com/quotes/50209-activism-is-my-rent-for-living-on-the-planet*.

23. Blastland and Spiegelhalter, *The Norm Chronicles*, 254.

24. Richard Sandomir, "Dr. Davida Coady, Medical Missionary, Dead at 80," *New York Times Obituaries*, May 13, 2018, 26.

25. Abraham Verghese, *Cutting for Stone* (New York: Random House, Vintage, 2009), 7.

Parenthood. We sometimes use the notion of calling to refer to trade, profession, and vocation, from the Latin *vocātiō*, a call or summons.

I was fortunate because I was able to find family life and professions—pastor, seminary professor, grassroots organizer, institute director, and activist—that helped satisfy deep callings. My steel-mill father had fewer choices. He never worked at a job that brought much personal satisfaction or happiness. His calling, his equally important social spirituality, was to provide, care for, and love his family, to help our spirits thrive no matter the personal cost. My mother's calling was to be a housewife, mother, and the best elementary school teacher in Butler County, Pennsylvania. Their family calling was to raise and educate their children.

Most of us feel specific callings—to raise families, do jury duty, maximize profit, create, invent, show up, manage, serve. In addition to our individual callings, we all have a generalized social calling by virtue of our social interdependence. We are called to treat one another decently (think: Otis Redding and Aretha Franklin's *R-E-S-P-E-C-T*) because we are all part of the same social fabric and dependent on one another.

We are not created physically, mentally, socially, or economically equal. Since equality as citizens exists (at least in theory), we are also called to active political participation, to maintain and enhance the possibility of the rights and benefits of citizenship and the democracy that makes it possible.

The definitive spiritual question is, "What sort of people do we want to be?" When we become clear that the answer is to be good stewards of the gifts we have received, we will nurture families, support public policies that address the needs of the world's most vulnerable people, and ensure the rights of all.

The kindling is the human condition. The sparks are the fire of disciplined commitment and work for people and earth, love, and justice. As we learn the disciplines of carrying the fire, the fire burns into us and becomes part of our self-identity—our souls, not just something we do, but who we are to our very core—a firebird who helps bring life out of ashes.

Being a good citizen has many seductions. There is a difference between "I *help* save people and the planet" and "I save them." Perhaps the most dangerous is the messianic reduction, "I can save the world." Sorry, it is always us, not just you or me.

"Are you one of the good guys?" "Do you eat people?"

"No, I am someone who helps carry the fire." *Helps!* I may carry it, but I do not carry it alone. *We* carry the fire, and that's part of the excitement.

"The Silent Seduction of Social Media"

How long I have been sitting frozen
frantic eyes skimming liquid crystal screens
where google and facebook and e-mail conspire
to narrow my vision, shrink my spirit, and
drown me facedown in shallow melt water.

How long I have been giving myself
to habits of cleverness and speed
skating slapdash over glistening pixels
on witty one-line blades or two
that rob me of curiosity and wonder.

How long I have been racing—
no entrechats or sleight-of-foot tricks for me,
no waiting to catch taut truth or Beauty
who always falls slowly, slowly,
slowly into patient outstretched imaginations.

How long I have closed my eyes
to poetry wafting gently through pinon
and evening chill and fire dancing
like San Miguel with neither sword nor balance
in his adobe chapel niche.

How long I have been dying
from hardening of heart by haste
blinded by piercing shards of impatience
while silence beckons and leaves
butterfly down to be caught by nimble dreams.

—Jim Benton

Part II

Citizen Spirituality

CHAPTER 3

We Are the End Game

At whose feet do you lay your freedom?

—*Fydor Dostoyevsky*

Power Is an Essential Part of Spirituality

Throughout history, people experienced powers that triggered spiritual experiences. Lightning bolts and crashing thunder suggested that the gods were angry. The endless orgasms of ocean waves on the rocks and sand suggested unseen sources. The moon hinted at mysterious rhythms in time and distances in space.

People could not prevent the insects that ravaged their crops or the droughts that led to starvation. They tried to make the rains come, the sun shine, the crops grow, but nature did what it wanted. Humans sensed a vitality and power that mysteriously transcended their ordinary powers. This power became a major source of spiritual experiences and practices—the activity of spirit gods in rain and rainbow, behind rocks, above clouds, and beneath crops.

They believed that something above, below, within, or beyond animated the natural phenomena they experienced. Powerful spirits, both good and evil, lurked in the rhythmic cycles of human and cosmic time, and in places that could be sacred or dangerous. The gods elicited terror, joy, awe, and pain—the fearsome destructiveness of chaos, death, and the unknown—but also, creativity, order, fecundity, beauty.

Since regular people often found themselves on the wrong side of natural and political powers, it was comforting to have a muscular Divine Spirit to counter their relative powerlessness. Gifts and sacrifices were offered to please or appease wrathful and vengeful spirits and rulers. Songs of devotion rose in acknowledgment of mysterious powers of nature, gods, and political rulers.

Religions and ritual practices existed, in part, to tame, mitigate, and routinize unpredictability of power and get it working in our behalf. Even today, people who are thoroughly secular might utter a silent prayer for help from a power greater than themselves in a situation spiraling dangerously out of control.

Sacred stories recounted both magical and mundane powers commanded by gods and political rulers, sometimes rolled into one bundle—holy wars, the divine right of kings, monuments, and temples. It is not surprising that scriptures include creation stories not only to answer where-did-it-all-come-from, but as an acknowledgment of the mysterious powers that apparently could create this complex something out of nothing.

When Obi-Wan Kenobi grasped Luke Skywalker's hand and solemnly intoned, "the Force be with you," people muttered to themselves, "Yeah. It's something like that, a force, a power for good that can help." The dark side in *Star Wars* is fear, anger, hatred; aggression that is passionate, seductive, and leads to evil acts. George Lucas intended "the Force be with you" as the positive blessing of a non-sectarian god.

Twelve-step groups call it a higher power. The AA *Big Book* says, "Lack of power (to quit drinking), that was our dilemma. We had to find a power by which we could live, and it had to be a *Power greater than* [more-than] *ourselves.*" Power (muscularity) is an intrinsic element in a fully realized spirituality. Power to overcome the demons of our inner drives. Power to survive and make living together habitable. Whether and how God exercises power in our daily life is an important question for another time. *We Carry the Fire* focuses on how we use our powers to carry the fire.

The Beatles sang, "All we need is love." Interpersonal love. But politics, the use of influence and power, is also a way of showing love to people both within and beyond arm's reach. When you engage politically, you can experience the satisfaction of using your personal power, your abilities, your moral values to see the gift of life rising out of the ashes where death would otherwise prevail.

We Advocated Changes

The stories that follow describe a seminary course where students used their collective power to bring about constructive social change. They read assigned books and pamphlets—ranging from the American Friends Service Committee to the National Rifle Association—about how to make change happen, and then they chose a project where they could learn how to bring about change by attempting to change something in the local community.

The stories illustrate how a small (typically a dozen), but energized group can use whatever power they have at hand to make change happen. Some of the projects succeeded. Some went sideways, but that too was a learning experience that helped the next time around. But none of these projects would have had a chance if just a dozen ordinary people with no extraordinary power, no budget, a short timeframe, and a lot of passion, thought, and energy had not bothered.

What makes these stories social and political spirituality is that they rise out of spiritual values and vision, inculcated by families, congregations, and other people. Values that said, "People should not have to endure unnecessary suffering." Values that said, "My life is intrinsically connected with other peoples' lives." Spiritual because of the sense of solidarity in working for justice together. Spiritual because we all want to feel that our lives connect with something larger (morethan) ourselves—"My piss-ant little life can make a difference in the real world," our calling, why we are here. Spiritual because we got results that added to the wellbeing of the human spirit.

Better Jail Conditions

One class decided to tackle conditions in the city jail. The Junior Bar was just completing a study of jail conditions, ready to make a report to city council. But their effort might die for lack of community interest. Our timing was just exactly right. *Lesson: timing is everything.* Timing is partly chosen and partly accidental, but it can make all the difference in small actions, elections, and social movements. Period.

The group chose a conflict strategy to dramatize conditions in the jail. We would picket city hall and press the case for change at the Monday morning city council meeting.[1] We were helped by Steve Larson, the urban minister, and Cliff Kirkpatrick, then executive director of the Community of Churches.[2] *Lesson: find the right people to help with your task.* Without them, we could not have done it.

As an independent citizens' group, not a seminary group, we could picket, make demands, and appear on the evening television news without being linked, we hoped, to the seminary or university and protect the school, not to mention our own sweet asses.

With much brainstorming and laughter, the group chose the name PORE—People Opposed to Repressive Enforcement. We were "for the PORE!" We had fun. Texas author and activist Jim Hightower (as I recall) described something as "more fun than eating ice cream in a bathtub naked." *Lesson: politics is sometimes an eating-ice-cream-while naked-in-a-bathtub experience.*

Steve, the urban minister, visited people in jail to document their complaints. We contacted an ACLU attorney to learn about our rights because we did not want accidentally to commit an infraction leading to arrest. We phoned local television and radio news departments to alert them to a Monday morning demonstration. We also got on the list of those who would make a presentation. *Lesson: get the facts; be disciplined.* Do not just act impulsively. Think through very carefully what you want to do. Prepare. Your parents were right. Do your homework.

Using city-generated statistics, we prepared a brochure that detailed problems in the jail—no toilet paper, a cold greasy egg sandwich for breakfast that had been cooked the night before and left

---

1. I say "we" because though I was the professor, I did not tell them what to do and always considered students my peers with different kinds of knowledge; for example, those who had just returned from service in Vietnam had experienced things I could barely imagine. The class made decisions by voting. It was important that they learned how to discover a relevant project, get to group consensus, plan, and take responsibility for implementation.

2. Cliff later became the stated clerk of the Presbyterian Church (U.S.A).

unrefrigerated till served early morning, cells designed for eighty sometimes holding 300, no blankets or mattresses, felons mixed in with misdemeanors. If arrested on the weekend for a minor infraction, you could be stuck in jail in rough company until a Monday morning hearing to determine whether they had enough evidence to hold you.

On Sunday evening we gathered at a Presbyterian Church office and fried ten dozen eggs in heavy grease, slapped them between slices of white bread, and let them set until morning. A reporter jammed a microphone into our faces so we could practice for Monday morning's hoped-for media. We made picket signs, including an "Eat at Joes" sandwich board, sandwiches in plastic baggies stapled onto a display board. *Lesson: be creative.*

Monday morning, leagues outside our comfort zone, we anxiously picketed city hall and handed cold egg sandwiches to city council members as they walked toward the building. Local media showed up in full force. *Lesson: be brave; stretch your personal boundaries.* Have the courage of your convictions.

Later that day we heard ourselves interviewed on radio and saw our demonstration on television. It was news because this medium-sized conservative city was unaccustomed to public demonstrations. What works in a town may not work in a big city or a different era.

The students made a presentation to the city council. One class member, who was also a therapist, used his skills to goad an opposing city council member into a foolish outburst, which only made the council member look silly and our case stronger, though it probably cost the therapist a city contract. The council referred the matter to committee.

The local newspapers carried a picture of our protest. Headlines shouted, "City Jail Conditions Protested" and "Jail Termed 'Inhumane.'" The next day: "City Jail Chief Blames Sorry 1938 Facilities" and listed PORE's charges. Much to our surprise, the chief jailer and the police were mostly on our side because they worked there and wanted better jail conditions too. But better conditions depended on more money, and the city and county governments held the purse strings.

So, we wrote letters to the editor and continued lobbying behind the scenes. *Lessons: media coverage can make a difference, and you never know with certainty who your allies or opponents are until they show up.*

During our demonstration we had handed out pamphlets inviting people to call our number and join. A stranger showed up at a classroom meeting. When Steve arrived, he recognized the newcomer as a city undercover policeman and greeted the officer by name. The officer hastily headed out the door. The city now knew who we were.

We were anxious to get on with it, lest it drag out past the end of the semester and our group disperse. By the early 1970s, college presidents had figured out that the best strategy to disperse a protest was to "delay until summer vacation." So, Cliff from the Community of Churches mounted a behind-the-scenes effort to lobby individual members of the council.

More newspaper headlines: "Jail Study Panel to Seek Changes." Then, "City Council Adopts Jail Improvements." When the subcommittee report was released, the council agreed to hot meals, mattresses, and blankets for the steel slab bunks, to bring in a judge Sunday morning to clear out Saturday night drunks, and to post the jail rules bilingually.

More headlines: "Jail Reform Actions Leave Much Undone." But: "These moves take care of some of the more deplorable conditions that have existed at the jail. . . . Members of PORE (People Opposed to Repressive Enforcement) and other concerned citizens are to be congratulated for their compassion and tenacity in pressing for needed reforms."

There were delays. "Council Puts Off Action on Drunks: Cost Questioned." But four years later, I went to that jail to get someone released. The blankets, mattresses, and bilingual rules for visiting hours were still there. Change happened and continued to benefit those who passed through that system. It was not a giant leap for humankind, but then the whole effort was only that of a dozen seminarians, allied with Urban Ministry and the Community of Churches, in a single three-credit course during a single semester.

We had great fun as well as the satisfaction of helping make changes happen. More than thirty years later, when I bumped into Cliff at a meeting, his first gleeful words were, "Do you remember that time we changed conditions in the city jail?"

Experiences like this are deeply meaningful because they connect us with other people, help people who are suffering a terrible time in their lives. We also helped the jailers, brought a little justice to the system, and added to the sum of human goodness. The people who rotate through that jail do not even know that we exist. Our satisfaction comes not from anyone saying thanks, but from knowing that we made a difference, however small, through political engagement.

A lot of factors must work together for an effort like this to be successful. But that time it worked, in large part because of the creativity and bravery of the students. It was a spiritual work, a spiritual experience, and the results enlarged the human spirit.

Handicap Access

The following year's students decided, despite my expressed doubts, to address handicap access at the seminary, a local congregation, and the university. At that time, the notion of special handicap access was just gaining traction, especially in conservative parts of the country.

We gathered articles and an accessibility checklist from the National Paraplegia Foundation. As a youth, I had delivered the *Butler Eagle* to the parsonage where Jim Grey, the executive director of the local branch of the Paraplegia Foundation, had grown up. Sometime after moving to Texas, Jim was in a club where someone started shooting. He was not the target, but he was injured and lived out his life in his wheelchair, serving other persons with disabilities (social spirituality).

The students who chose to work with a congregation met with the property committee. Through a series of meetings and discussions, the church committee gradually decided to follow guidelines for people with handicaps and improve ramps, bathrooms, door widening, and a designated parking area.

The group focused on the seminary crafted a list of desired changes, sent them to the student government, and lobbied the dean and faculty. The students also used a wheelchair and crutches to get a personal feeling for the experience and demonstrate to others the difficulties of negotiating the seminary building where most classrooms were on the second floor, but there were no ramps or elevators.

A faculty member filed a complaint against me after noticing students' giggling at the awkwardness of carrying someone down two sets of steps in a wheelchair. She said, rightly, that real people in wheelchairs do not find steps funny. At some point the dean apparently made the complaint disappear.

On the university side, students drafted a bill and presented it to the Student House of Representatives, and it was duly reported in the student newspaper. They also took their complaints and proposed changes to the vice chancellor. The Student House approved the bill, but the vice chancellor was unhappy. Some of the information the students presented was outdated. And since we had not asked, we were unaware of changes that the university was already planning to make, or so they said. *Lesson: if you are going to lobby, be careful to get your facts straight or you will look unprepared, foolish, and you may delay rather than accelerate progress toward your goals.*

The vice chancellor wrote a long letter to the Student House of the university listing things the university had already done, planned to do, and expressing frustration at our effort. We responded with an equally long letter apologizing for our mistakes and suggesting that, measured by the Aristotelian criterion of "best under the circumstances," the university was apparently trying, but that by Aristotle's more stringent criterion, "the best absolutely," they weren't doing very well, and cited evidence to support that claim.

A few weeks later, I noticed that curb corners on the streets in the immediate vicinity of the seminary had suddenly been smashed into rubble. Just the corners. Just around the seminary. I imagined students swinging sledgehammers in the middle of the night to break down the corners so that the new corners would be ramped for wheelchairs. I figured "Don't ask, don't tell" and to this day do not know what happened.

What I do know is that by the end of the semester, the church had begun the changes required for handicap access, and the seminary had ramped curbs and added a new handicap-accessible seminary apartment as well as an accessible bathroom. The administration, of course, contended that our activities had nothing to do with the changes. The students did not care what the administration said. They wanted results, not medals.

A student summarized what she had learned:

1. Increased our awareness of handicap concerns. (I almost let the air out of the tires of a truck parked in a handicap slot at a restaurant.)

2. Change is never easy. It often results in pain.

3. Even safe issues have a "bear in the woods." People are easily threatened.

4. Information has power, but quantitative information has a premium value.

5. Bottom line is dollars.

6. You have more power in presence than on paper or by telephone.

7. It takes time to go to meetings. It takes tenacity.

8. Do good research on the issue. Identify the political structure. Identify allies.

9. Know the political realities of the institutional structure you are dealing with.

School for Undocumented Children

Another class decided to work alongside in solidarity with people who were trying to make it possible for undocumented workers' children to attend public schools without having to pay tuition. Undocumented children, mostly Mexican and Central American, had long attended schools alongside Texas-born children, but the legislature had passed a bill that terminated state funds for the education of children of undocumented workers.

Our first strategy was to try to convince members of the school board to make an exception and carry the children without state reimbursement. We familiarized ourselves with their backgrounds and status, general leanings, and who they listened to. It quickly became clear that little could be expected from that quarter. *Lesson: stasis, status, and money prevail.* We had no standing in the community and certainly no money.

The class discovered that a small band of local people was running a free school for undocumented workers' children in a church. Students met with a reporter from a newspaper and leaked information about the school. A few days later a Dallas newspaper front-page headline proclaimed, "'Night Schools' Sidestep Law to Help."

The article described a small group of people gathered in a "clandestine night meeting . . . hidden from public view," anonymous, but not to talk about drugs or pornography, but the "education of the estimated 500 children of undocumented workers in Fort Worth who are not permitted in public schools." Within a day, television news programs showed Hispanic children trying to study in makeshift classrooms. Again, media strategies were crucial.

The class, discouraged by the school board's continuing lack of response, decided to explore a legal challenge. A local attorney agreed to pursue the case *pro bono.* The class developed go-to-court fever. We boned up on INS citizenship requirements and policies.

We first had to find an undocumented parent willing to complain that her child was being denied fair treatment—not easy because an undocumented parent who goes public might be deported. A student told a local journalist about a woman who had been deported, leaving her children, ages six to fourteen behind. "The family lives in a dark, musty house on the North Side," began the article by Robert Seltzer.

I told the seminary dean that a class was about to sue the school board on behalf of undocumented children. He later referred to it as the day he was glad he was wearing brown pants. Yet, he was so strongly committed to academic freedom that he did not try to stop us. In enlisting an attorney, we had gained a sense of power and reality, but we lost control of the process. We learned that the issue was already before the Fifth Circuit Court in New Orleans and decided to wait until the court issued its judgment. Long after the semester ended, schools nationwide were required to admit undocumented children.

An endemic problem with the course was that when the semester ended, the project had to end. So, there were always questions about how ethically to drop a project that was unfinished. Several class members decided to build a coalition to carry on part of the work at the local level. With clergy support, they called a breakfast meeting that led to the Coalition of Good Neighbors. A student became a member of the steering committee; another took a position as a local urban minister and continued to work with the coalition on tutoring programs for newly arriving families. Still other students published their opinions in the "Voices of the People" column in the local newspaper.

We learned about current conditions, policies, and legal options, but did not change any laws or policies. *Lessons: When you participate, you may not win but you will learn more each time; you may influence if not change structures; and ethical endings count.*

Were these social justice projects just student pranks? They certainly were fun, and it felt good to be part of a wider group of students nation- and worldwide who were expressing their values through political activism. Some who took the course have gone on to decades of full- or part-time vocations in *conscientization*, social service, ministry, and advocacy. A former student recently wrote, "I want you to know the incredible amount of impact you had and have had on my life and ministry, which includes being a parish pastor, denominational leader, community organizer, and initiator of a service non-profit."

One student went on to work with women in the developing world, another to start a housing nonprofit in the United States, another to train to become a community organizer, still another to work as a substance abuse counselor in a Roman Catholic–sponsored halfway house, and many have made social service and social justice a central element in their ministry as laity or pastors in congregations.

It is not always easy to measure the amount of change that happens in society, but participation in political justice can build spiritual identity, which plays out over time, even generations when shared through families and other social relationships. The number of people who were helped and inspired remains unknown and uncountable.

Power as the Ability to Act

The first definition of power is "the ability to act." You have the power, the ability, to get up in the morning, to put jelly on your toast, make coffee, hug your loved ones.

Nobel laureate Amartya Sen and philosopher Martha Nussbaum describe our ability to act as "capabilities." They say that in our lives we have "alternative combinations of things a person is able to do or be— the various 'functionings' he or she can achieve," capabilities that "vary from such elementary matters as being well nourished and disease-free to more complex doings or beings, such as having self-respect, preserving human dignity, taking part in the life of the community."[3]

For a person to be free, they must be able to actualize these capabilities. You are not fully free if you are disease-ridden, malnourished, beset by thieves, being sold for a price, or unable to get an education, health care, and means of survival. You cannot achieve your maximum human potential unless certain basic human requirements are met, first among them the basic ability to live and to express yourself purposively. You cannot be fully empowered if you do not have enough to eat and the ability to participate meaningfully in the community.

---

3. Martha Nussbaum and Amartya Sen, eds., *The Quality of Life* (New Delhi: Oxford University Press, 1993), 3, 30. See also Amartya Sen's *The Idea of Justice* (Cambridge: Harvard University Press, Belknap Press, 2009). Nussbaum proposes a summary of her "thick vague theory of the good" as she lists the essential functions required to constitute a human life, and therefore the things that we aim to achieve, in "Human Functioning and Social Justice," *Political Theory*, May 1992, 202–46.

Richard Rorty writes, "My candidate for the most distinctive and praiseworthy human capacity is our ability to trust and to cooperate with other people, and in particular to work together so as to improve the future."[4] The force is our ability to act, our creativity in the face of fixed ideas and structures, our ability to affect changes in our lives and the wider world when we work with others. Apathy and death are the thieves that, in mid-morning, steal our power, our ability to think, feel, and act.

Just as it matters which more-than you seek, it matters how you use your powers—whether you act for goodness or evil for yourself and others. And the power that is generally available to people in democratic societies happens most dramatically through politics. Politics amplifies the power of the individual to become "we the people." But it takes a lot of us working together to bring change. We are kayaks in relation to large corporations and governments that are like ocean liners and aircraft carriers—big, slow, and hard to divert. It takes 40,000 regular people contributing $25 each to offset the $1 million contribution of a single billionaire.

For the first time in human history, we the people also have the social and political power that previous societies attributed to a god or gods—to be the destroyer of worlds. The choice is ours, well, and nature's (climate change, asteroids). Ours is the spiritual task of using power for good. We are the force, but we do not force. Our work is to discern and work for moral results within democratic norms and the rule of law. Democracy is fragile and continuously needs renewal.

Power in its largest social setting is the venue of politics, the ability to influence more than each of us can do individually. We join with others to have enough muscle to make large-scale changes. Politics is an essential vehicle through which we can help create the common good by working in solidarity with people who are often of other faiths, races, and cultures. The moral exercise of power is a spiritual process that can provide spiritual experiences.

---

4. Richard Rorty, *Philosophy and Social Hope* (London: Penguin Books, 1999), xiii.

A Mayor's Thoughts on Power, by Jim Rurak

I wrote my friend, theologian and politician Jim Rurak,

> When I talk about spirituality, it has difficult challenges that
> includes your time campaigning and in office. I believe that you,
> Kathy [his wife], along with others, worked your tail off to become
> elected, and then did as much good as you could while in office.
> That work was a spiritual work in that it was a striving to
> improve the human condition, the human spirit, to move the chunk
> of humanity that you had access to, forward. It did not feel 'spir-
> itual' most of the time, but it was a spiritual work that delivered
> spiritual results, no matter how compromised they were by the
> political/bureaucratic process.
>
> And, if you, further, imagine that your striving is part of that
> great body of human witnesses, in every country, over all time, of
> every religion and race who sacrifices for the good of humanity and
> the planet, then perhaps that can bring spiritual feelings as well as
> spiritual results.

Jim wrote back,

> I do see the work you did and do, the work we do and did, as spiri-
> tual in that it serves the greater human good. But I do acknowledge
> sin. A lot of what we did and do serves ourselves. I do believe that
> in our ambiguous efforts there are many moments when our lim-
> ited and even selfish motives are transformed by our sense of serv-
> ing something greater, when we act then for that greater purpose, in
> short when we are converted.
>
> Conversion isn't just a come-to-Jesus moment confined to a
> religious setting. It happens all the time, and these actions, personal
> and social, are spiritual and the experience of them is of something
> greater than us working in and through us. Call this what you will,
> but acknowledge its power to change us from those who think
> they know best to those who are bettered by it when they serve it.
> And these experiences and actions do both give us and define that

direction which collectively serves that "higher power." But having actual, political power is not antithetical to serving a higher power.

At many times and in many places through history, monarchs ruled by God's authority and were subject to no earthly authority. There was an aura around the monarch that no mere human force should penetrate. Supposedly, democratic revolutions changed all this. Power and authority come from the consent of the governed. No magic surrounds elected officials. In fact, if today there is anything special surrounding them, it is the smell of snake oil.

True as this may be as seen from the outside, the experience from the inside, from being elected to wield power, is a different story.

I was elected Mayor of Haverhill, Massachusetts in 1993. The office is that of a "real mayor," in that there is no city manager and the mayor is the sole authority to hire and fire city employees. The mayor is the chief financial officer and, in our special case, the "owner" of a hospital and a nursing home, and the mayor is elected directly by the people for a set term; there is no recall provision.

Once elected, then, the mayor of a mid-sized city has a lock on real power. It is not the power over millions, like that of a president, governor, or large city "mayor." But it is direct power over policies and people that has both immediate and long-term impacts.

Once elected, my life changed. People I once may have looked up to now called me 'mayor.' They deferred to me in public and rarely challenged me in private. City department heads who knew their jobs asked for my consent and vied for my approval.

It wasn't just an ego boost; it was a real shocker, one that I felt I had to match with all my personal, intellectual, and political abilities.

If I messed up (it was only my first of four two-year terms), I'd be on a downward spiral. That is where the consent of the governed comes in. But one thing made it work, even produced something of the feeling of invincibility: wielding power. Yes, try to be fair, moral, and reasonable, but, above all, wield power. Power, wielded effectively, breeds more power and more respect. And, when you mess up, you gain power by admitting it and facing the music—just as a king might seek penance from a bishop.

So, my simple conclusion from having had such power is that while it now might be derived from a democratic process, the experience and effect of wielding it differs little from when it was thought to have been derived from God. A president, senator, governor, mayor may fall from grace more quickly than a king, by the verdict of the electorate, but when in power, power is power. The more you use it, the more you accomplish, the better it feels.

Let me be clear. I am not talking about how you acquire power, nor about how you maintain it, nor about whether you wield it morally or not. I am talking about how it feels when you have it and use it. It feels magical. You say, "Do this," and roads get built, schools too, laws get enforced, things get bought and sold. No matter how hard you had to work to get it and maintain it, when you use it, you feel the "wand" in your hand turn dreams into facts.

That is why few people willingly give up power. Usually, you lose it because the "wand" turned you into a sorcerer's apprentice. You unleashed forces beyond your control, and they came back to overwhelm you. Or, more prosaically, people want more or less than you give them. Or you get into trouble. All of that is a topic for a much larger analysis.

The experience of power that I've described raises only one question. Is it good? My answer is an unequivocal, "Yes." You need not be a mayor or a king to experience power. But you must be something, somebody. One of the most powerful people I've known was also one of the most humble.

He was a carpenter who knew what he was doing and knew what he didn't know. He would never tell an electrician what to do, but if an electrician tried to tell him how to do his job, a wall as strong as that in China went up. And he kept going at his own pace. The building went up, straight, true, and square. He loved every minute of it. Another is a poet. She loves every minute of trying to make a poem work. She is delighted when it finally does. Because of this, she not only creates great poems, she appreciates great poems greatly.

You can describe power as "the ability to act," but the experience of power is in the acting and feeling yourself as the agency of accomplishment. From Karl Marx to Adam Smith, the root experience is the same. It is to feel human, to make a mark that befits your abilities. For that simple reason, power produces both good and evil. But the experience of power in itself is a great part of what it means to be alive.

Power in itself is good. It is spiritual and serves a higher power when it is held accountable to the purposes and people from which it is derived. When those purposes and people are accountable to the higher power that frees them from their selfish ambitions, then the life for which we're meant to live is lived.

Politics Is the Oxygen of Community Life

When people say, "I don't get involved in politics," that's like saying, "I don't get involved in breathing air." Politics is part of the social oxygen that gives us life. We are actively or passively, by commission or omission, involved in politics. There are politics in family relationships, in social groups, at work, in all parts of our social life, though the focus here is on politics in public life.

When people say, "I don't do politics," consider responding, "But, politics does you." Politics in public life affects us whether we choose to participate or not. The choice not to take an active role leaves the decisions up to other people who may not have your, your family, or your community's best interests in mind. In fact, many who have enormous power care mainly about themselves.

Author James Patterson wrote, "These days people all around the world are angry about and suspicious of the super-rich and powerful. . . . we ought to be. To put it simply some people think they can operate outside the law. And that's what they do."[5] Or at least many who have huge amounts of wealth and power do.

The workings of politics are as *mysterious* as those of social interactions—difficult to understand and hidden behind appearances.

---

5. James Patterson, "Author's Note," in James Patterson and John Connolly with Tim Malloy, *Filthy Rich* (New York: Little, Brown and Company, 2016), x.

How can my tiny effort make any difference? Politics is certainly *meaningful* for citizen participants, whether lobbying, running for, or holding office. Politics is the way we achieve results that are *more-than* any one individual can achieve; results that affect whole communities and the world. Public politics is, by definition, *mighty/muscular*, and at its best *moral*, with distinctive political *methods* and *memories* of historical events crystalized in laws and statues, procedures, heroines, monuments, and traditions that influence decision making.

Participation in public life is a spiritual calling, sometimes destroying individuals and degrading society, sometimes saving lives and bringing greater wholeness to our collective life. In a democracy, political action by individuals is the way to counterbalance abusive power, especially with and on behalf of those who are most victimized. We are dependent on the participation of one another.

The Declaration of Independence Was Also a Declaration of Dependence

"Americans" are justly proud of our independence. When public policy tradeoffs are made in the United States, freedom often prevails over equality, and freedom is a wonderful gift from the many who have sacrificed to establish and maintain it. However, the Declaration of Independence was also a Declaration of Dependence: mutual dependence among widely separated colonies to fight and die for something they believed in but which lacked a clear future. In Benjamin Franklin's well-known words: "We must, indeed, all hang together, or most assuredly we shall all hang separately."

The former colonies were not cohesive after the Revolutionary War. Some thought that Royalists, loyal to the crown, would still seek ways to secede and reconnect with England. And the Southern states did secede less than a hundred years later, or as I call it, "one Mary Catherine" later, since that's what I decided to denote one-hundred-year units after my mother became a centenarian.

Great Britain had the largest army and navy in the world, capable of invading and blockading the colonies. We received assistance from the French, and one of the big concerns was whether the colonies would simply be trading Britain for France as colonial masters. Without the French navy, supplies, and financial assistance, we might not have achieved independence, so the colonists were dependent on France as well as one another. In today's interlocked trade, travel, and tech world, there is even less individual or national self-sufficiency. The struggle to manage our long-declared independence, dependence, and interdependence continues.

The Beginning:

That to secure these rights, Governments are instituted among Men (sic), deriving their just powers from the consent of the governed, . . . with a firm reliance on the protection of divine Providence, we mutually pledge to each other our Lives, our Fortunes and our sacred Honor.

—Declaration of Independence. July 4, 1776

The Middle:

We the People of the United States, in Order to form a more perfect Union, establish Justice, insure domestic Tranquility, provide for the common defence (sic), promote the general Welfare, and secure the Blessings of Liberty to ourselves and our Posterity, do ordain and establish this Constitution for the United States of America.

—Preamble to the Constitution
of the United States of America, 1787

The End Game:

It is rather for us to be here dedicated to the great task remaining before Us—that from these honored dead we take increased devotion to that cause for which they gave the last full measure of devotion . . . and that government of the people, by the people, for the people, shall not perish from the earth.

—Abraham Lincoln, Gettysburg, November 19, 1863

An inscription on the wall behind the nineteen-foot sculpture of Abraham Lincoln at the Lincoln Memorial in Washington, DC, says Lincoln saved the union. But he knew that no one person could or did. He was dependent on others, as he said, "From these honored dead we take increased devotion to that cause for which they gave the last full measure of devotion."

Yes, *they* died. They died at Gettysburg, at Lexington and Concord, on the beaches of Normandy, the Battle of the Bulge, Iwo Jima, the Chosin Reservoir, Khe Sanh, Kamdesh. They also were killed on a balcony in Memphis, in a motorcade in Dallas, in protests, in barrios, in the 'hood. Others lived, worked, and sacrificed for a government "of the people, by the people, and for the people." "*By* the people"—not, as it too often seems, "buy the people." We are the end game. And yet . . .

People Avoid Politics

Many people dislike and disparage politics because they see self-aggrandizement, partisan posturing, public bickering, treachery, bureaucracy, and corruption. When Glenda Jackson, who won two Oscars and also served in the British parliament, was asked who had the biggest egos, politicians or actors, she said, "The egos that I saw in Parliament wouldn't have been tolerated for thirty seconds in the theater."[6]

Some people ignore politics because it is all they can do to earn a living and take care of their family. Others are distracted from active citizenship by the toys, trinkets, and perks of contemporary life that they think they need. Some are distracted by popular spiritualities that reduce spirituality to individual bliss, escape, inner peace.

People say that voting and politics do not make a difference. The issues seem too complex and intractable. The forces arrayed seem too large, the processes obscure and messy. Politics sometimes seems like a set of games other people play somewhere else that have little effect on our lives, and only get our attention when we feel harmed.

---

6. Belinda Luscombe, "11 Questions," *Time*, April 16, 2018, 56.

Every human activity is subject to chaos and corruption. "In every man, of course a demon lies hidden—the demon of rage, the demon of lustful heat at the screams of the tortured victim, the demon of lawlessness let off the chain" (Ivan Karamazov to his brother Alyosha).[7] But when it comes to public sector politics, bad decisions are multiplied because the decisions made by governments have an enormous influence on people and events—Mao's "Politics is war without bloodshed while war is politics with bloodshed."

Absolute power does tend to corrupt absolutely, but as community organizers point out, powerlessness also corrupts absolutely. People lose a sense of shared citizenship when their voices are not heard, and rulers make policies that are not in the public interest, especially when they impact "The Last, The Lost, The Least" (song by Relient K).

For all the problems, we do expect decisions to get made, fire trucks, snowplows and school buses to arrive, pot holes to be filled, rules of the road, dependability of contracts, vulnerable people cared for, schools that teach, hospitals that heal, courts that protect, war prevented. We expect to be shielded from some large forces of evil, and good promoted for individuals, communities, and the natural world. In an uncertain world, it is our role to tip the balance toward that good.

Ed Chambers quotes Sheldon Wolin: "By politicalness I mean our capacity for developing into beings who know and value what it means to participate in and be responsible for the care and improvement of our common and collective life." Chambers adds, "Developing our politicalness means that we know and value what it means to have power. . . . Exercising politicalness means that we participate in something larger than our individual projects. . . . The problem is that average Americans don't see politicalness as a vocation. . . . Living out our religious and democratic values requires that public life be part of our citizenship and mission."[8]

---

7. Fyodor Dostoyevsky, *The Brothers Karamazov*, tr. Constance Garnett (New York: The Lowell Press, 2009), 265. Retrieved from *https://www.gutenberg.org/files/28054/28054-pdf.pdf*.

8. Edward T. Chambers, *Roots for Radicals: Organizing for Power, Action, and Justice* (New York: Continuum, 2003), 70–71.

People also complain that government takes too much of their money, though they are happy to cash any government check with their name on it. We do have to be cautious, vigilant, about governmental intrusion in our private lives—our civil liberties, our individual understandings of morality, our religious freedom, as well as our so-called private wealth.

Governments, like corporations or any large institution, waste money as well as spend it well. The largest item in the federal budget is for defense, and that is probably where the greatest waste occurs. But face it, you and I probably waste a high percentage of our income too. Do I really need whatever it is that I desire, or just want? And, when policy makers say we cannot afford this or that social program, do they ever look at the full picture of American spending?

- In 2017, consumers spent much more on jewelry and watches ($82.5 billion) than the federal government spent on the Food Stamp Program ($68 billion).[9] The program gave benefits to an average forty-six million Americans. I hear complaints about the cost of food stamps but not about jewelry and watches.

- In the United States, bars and nightclubs generate about $24 billion in revenues each year," and that doesn't include the alcohol we buy from liquor stores, whereas the federal government spent $5.4 billion on the Special Supplemental Program for Women, Infants, and Children (WIC) which served nearly seven million people in 2018.[10]

- The Children's Health Insurance Program (CHIP), which serves nearly two million children, cost the federal government about $12 billion in fiscal year 2018. CHIP provides routine check-ups,

9. "This How Much Americans Spend on Jewelry and Watches," Edhan Golan, May 13, 2019; "The US Jewelry State of the Market Report," *https://www.edahngolan.com/so-how-much-do-we-spend-on-jewelry-and-watches/*; "Food Stamp Costs Hit Seven-Year Low," Breitbart, *https://www.breitbart.com/politics/2017/12/12/food-stamp-hit-seven-year-low/*.

10. Brandongaille, 22 Bar and Nightclub Industry Statistics and Trends, *https://brandongaille.com/22-bar-and-nightclub-industry-statistics-and-trends/*. *https://www.hhs.gov/about/budget/fy2018/budget-in-brief/cms/chip/index.html*.

immunizations, prescriptions, dental and vision care, inpatient and outpatient hospital care, laboratory, X-ray and emergency services for children. By comparison, "Americans spent about $15 billion for carbonated soft drinks, many of which contribute to obesity."[11] In 2017, there was a big fight in Congress as to whether to boost funding for CHIP, but little, if any, mention of limiting soft drinks.

- We spend ten times as much on shoes as on official foreign assistance. By one estimate, tobacco users "spend more than $320 billion a year on cigarettes and health care for smoking-related illnesses."[12] Yet, nearly 700 million people in developing countries live in extreme poverty, living on less than the U.S. equivalent of $1.90 a day.

We vote with our dollars as well as with our ballots. Watches are a good thing, and the tradeoffs are more complex than these comparisons suggest. I enjoy a martini as much as the next person, but if pressed, I would admit that the school lunch and WIC programs are more important than an evening at a restaurant. It is just that we do not think about it. Governments are convenient targets while our individual actions are "just normal consumer behavior." Perhaps we should stop to examine "normal consumer behavior."

Decisions about the public good are decisions made by the body politic, whether consciously or unconsciously, by action or inaction, passion or apathy. The Good Samaritan story, so often cited in religious circles, is both helpful and unhelpful. We do want to help the person whom we see "by the side of the road," but we also need to influence the policies of governments so that we help the millions who live by roads that we will never see.

Today's Good Samaritan does acts of justice through political action as well as acts of charity. It is not about guilt, but about

---

11. Sheila Marikar, "Fizz Is Now Big Biz," *New York Times Sunday Styles*, July 14, 2019, 1.

12. Adam McCann, "The Real Cost of Smoking," WalletHub, January 15, 2020, *https://wallethub.com/edu/the-financial-cost-of-smoking-by-state/9520/*.

responsibility. Or maybe productive guilt. Or maybe repentance and making amends. Or maybe just being realistic about our own good fortune and the relatively poor luck of the "other." Theologize however you wish, just do it.

Our Soul Brought Us Here

Senate Leader Charles Schumer was a Harvard student who had never heard of 1967's presidential contender Eugene McCarthy when a fellow student invited him to a political rally in New Hampshire where Schumer "caught the bug." "He loved the excitement of politics, along with the camaraderie and the sense of being involved in great events."[13]

Participation in the larger civic and political structures of our lives is, in one sense, the highest form of human activity, because this participation enables us to express our knowledge and interests to help the body politic. Millions live or die, thrive or fail to survive, depending on large-scale political decisions in which we can play an important role.

Politics is supremely important for the life and death struggle of individuals, peoples, and nations. We cannot have good communities unless they are composed of good people, but we cannot have good people unless we have good communities. Each supports and is dependent on the other. Enlarging the realm of family and civic goodness is a spiritual calling.

On May 17, 1968, in Catonsville, Maryland, nine war resisters removed files from the Selective Service Office which identified 378 young men to be conscripted to fight in the Vietnam War. They dumped them in the street below, poured homemade napalm over them, and set them on fire. They submitted to arrest, trial, and prison sentences, though some went underground to encourage further resistance before they reported to prison.

---

13. Elizabeth Kolbert, "Can Chuck Schumer Check Donald Trump?" *New Yorker*, March 27, 2017, *https://www.newyorker.com/magazine/2017/03/27/can-chuck-schumer-check-donald-trump.*

At the trial of the Catonsville Nine, Daniel Berrigan testified in response to the court's unwillingness to judge the morality of the war:

> Your honor, we are having great difficulty in trying to adjust to the atmosphere of a court from which the world is excluded, and the events that brought us here are excluded. . . . Our moral passion was excluded. It is as though we were subjects of an autopsy, were being dismembered by people who wondered whether or not we had a soul. We are sure that we have a soul. It is our soul that brought us here. It is our soul that got us into trouble.[14]

"Nine Kitchen Matches"

The wind, like history, blows as it will,
carries the ashes from the dusty street.
Nine kitchen matches, nine lovers
of *Peace and Decency and Unity and Love*
kindled the fire that was kindled in them,
mysterious as lightning, enchanting as moonlight,
animating them with the power to act
for those whose deaths were demanded
by faceless, cold-hearted, patrons of power.

Crumpled and black, thin as butterfly wings,
papers of war drift away into the past
as if the fire were snuffed out,
its light extinguished, doused
by the cold futility of souls burning within,
of hearts aflame with life,
in a worldwide Ice Age of death.
Even the cruel staying power

---

14. Daniel Berrigan, *The Trial of the Catonsville Nine* (Boston: Beacon, 1970), 113–14.

of homemade napalm cannot preserve
the light and heat of their fiery witness.

Powerless criminals ignite resistance
to criminal powers, voice moral passion
to cold steel exclusion of passion from policy,
life from law. In time their voices
and the ashes of their signal fire
move underground. Entombed, perhaps,
but not. They arise from below
kindle new flames among the people,
anoint them with the fire of resistance,
the power of love.

Even cruel napalm, flowing slowly, sticking
tenaciously, extruding its flaying terror
indiscriminate over all, cannot outlive the light
that is not the sun, incendiary giver and taker of life.
Like the naked napalmed girl we know,
arms extended in terror, fleeing down a road of war,
carving a path in our memory, images endure.
Photographs and films, stories and tombstones. Names
etched on the dark granite wound at the center of power,
reflecting the power of each, the remains of death,
the flames of life.

At Catonsville, a single fire was lit
by nine kitchen matches and one small batch
of homemade napalm. It burned three hundred papers
ordering young men to death. And soon
it was dust swept away by history's wind
and orderly brooms that burned children

as casually as paper. From prison cells
and catacombs, in pulpits and protests,
the ashes of nine arose, striking new sparks,
burning new images, kindling new power
to resist the old. Nine matches, ninety marches,
nine hundred candles, nine thousand fires.

—Jim Benton

CHAPTER 4

By the People

When we are dreaming alone it is only a dream.
When we dream together, it is the beginning of reality.

—Brazilian Archbishop Hélder Pessoa Câmara

Politics Is a Multiplier

Real involvement in the political process beyond voting is an uphill climb for many people. Religious people may be very political at work, but engaging in the nonstop process of supporting democracy seems more distant. Many faith groups tend to be personalistic, focused on individuals, and hence prefer charity as a solution to social problems. The Jewish tradition has paid more attention than some other traditions to social justice, perhaps because of the emphasis on the nation.

In 1962, just out of seminary, I was assigned a start-up mission, Good Shepherd Lutheran Church in Brunswick, Maine. The denomination provided thirty Bibles, thirty hymnals, fifty folding chairs, money to buy a desk and mimeograph machine (look it up), a church under construction, a parsonage, a $4,500 salary with benefits, a short-term operational subsidy, and debt for the buildings. So, I swept the floors, unfolded the chairs, set out the hymnals, and knocked on doors.

That fall, while I was focused on starting a congregation, other people were preparing to destroy whole cities, and our lives as well as our buildings depended on their decisions. The Brunswick Naval Air Station's maritime patrol planes photographed Russian missiles on ships headed to Cuba as the Missile Crisis unfolded. At least one commanding officer was in a plane in the air 24/7, ready to go.

A Soviet submarine commander, fearing attack, wanted to arm the sub's nuclear tipped torpedoes. But another commander refused to go along with a decision that could have led to thermonuclear war between the United States and the Soviets. It has been said that this was the most dangerous moment in world history. The commander who blocked the arming was Vasili Alexandrovich Arkhipov. *National Geographic* wrote, "You (and Almost Everyone You Know) Owe Your Life to This Man."[1] War was prevented by a few key individuals in military and political positions.

We stored a few cans of soup, tuna, and soda in the basement. How naïve and ill-informed. While some religious people were worrying about the tortures of hell, the Missile Crisis symbolized the more proximate hovering horrors of history. There was a problem with my knowledge, priorities, and sense of scale—a problem shared by many people today. We were not bad people, just consumed by everydayness, by seductive and morally numbing cultural values, and an appalling lack of concern for larger realities that, nonetheless, affected our lives.

During those years, U.S. involvement in Vietnam was on the verge of doubling and tripling. The young officers at the naval air station were eager to go to Vietnam because "that's what we signed up for" and "that's where the action and promotions are." Most Americans did not know where Vietnam was. History was speeding up, and many of us were clueless about things that were crucial to human survival and well-being.

Over time, the moral values taught by religious congregations can inform or even overcome the politics of the moment, but if the missiles fell, millions of us would not have a long term. Do not bother digitizing the family pictures because none of your family may survive to look at them.

When 1960's discussions turned to racism, church people said that the solution was to change individual attitudes. Change comes from many directions, but this solution ignored embedded institutional racism. It increasingly became clear that big change required

---

1. Robert Krulwich, "You (and Almost Everyone You Know) Owe Your Life to This Man," *National Geographic*, https://news.nationalgeographic.com/2016/03/you-and-almost-everyone-you-know-owe-your-life-to-this-man/.

influencing social and political structures, as well as paying attention to individual people—*Brown v. the Board of Education*, as well as listening to Mrs. Brown. How many times we have heard, "Get your act together first." I have worked with a lot of dysfunctional social activists who would have been more effective if they had spent more time dealing with their personal demons and dysfunctions. Yet, with decades of experience I feel confident in saying that we never perfectly get our act together (think: Garden of Eden). If personal good-feeling is our main focus, we'll never get around to important actions that help save the rest of the world as well as ourselves.

Another typical response to societal problems is charity—volunteer, dig wells for people in need, food banks, soup kitchens, cancer walks, Habitat houses, and contribute money to buy chickens and goats for needy people abroad. Charitable efforts absolutely do make a difference. Local, national, and international agencies could not operate without donations and volunteers. These agencies can provide real help to people in need. But never enough people act to make changes of the scale required, and government decisions can wipe out tens of thousands of local efforts.

Beginning in 1997, Julia (Butterfly) Hill set a world record 738 days living high in the canopy of a California redwood to protest clear-cutting of ancient forest. "She endured ninety-mile-per-hour winds, El Niño downpours, almost constant damp and cold, and deprivation (she lived mostly on raw fruits and vegetables and used a plastic-lined bucket for a toilet)." Meanwhile the Pacific Lumber Corporation continued clearing 10,000 acres of redwoods. Her courage was admirable, and her story still amazes and inspires.

However, an Earth Day article in *Newsweek* pointed out that, "Saving a tree only to lose a forest, her protest against logging forced activists to confront a disturbing possibility; that individual actions on behalf of the environment pale beside the actions of big business and big government." Environmentalist Barry Commoner pointed out that well-meaning people don't always take adequate account of the effectiveness of their actions: "A single decision by the chairman of Royal Dutch/Shell has a greater impact on the health of the planet" than all those who participate in Earth Day activities.[2]

An essential path to a relatively just, peaceful, and sustainable society where the rule of law prevails is also the most direct one—strengthening families, education, economies, democracy, and justice through political engagement. The Cuban Missile Crisis had its origins and solutions in individual decisions and actions that were magnified with great force in politics and public policies. The outcome could have seriously set back the human spirit. My colleague Michael Kuchinsky and I have coffee mugs from NASFAM, The National Smallholder Farmers' Association of Malawi that say, "The Future Belongs to the Organized." So it does.

The stories that follow illustrate some additional ways I have seen fires sparked and carried. One powerful way to be involved is to run for and win public office. But, running for public office is expensive, requires huge sacrifices, not everyone is naturally good at it, and most people lose. One of the best ways for most of us to be involved is to actively contribute our time and money in support of candidates, political parties, neighborhood, and issue advocacy groups.

The stories that follow are not world shaking or headline making, mostly just the stories of people with no extraordinary powers who tried to be part of "by the people." The examples are organized around types of involvement that are larger than the student projects: lobbying an agency, neighborhood organizing, faith-based community organizing, and movement politics. Society needs effective civic institutions at all levels for democracy to be sustained. For the top levels to work well, there must be a network of sustaining efforts and organizations at all levels. And people who learn their basic political skills at the local levels sometimes use those skills to migrate to higher office.

---

2. Sharon Begley, "The Battle for Planet Earth," *Newsweek*, April 24, 2000, 50–51.

A cautionary note: be careful about demonizing those who disagree with you as so many people are doing in this highly partisan time. I have an acquaintance who disagrees with me on most national political issues. From my point of view, many of the political arguments he adduces are the result of media propaganda and demonstrably untrue. And he thinks the same is exactly true for me.

Yet, every morning he gets up and goes to spend several hours sitting with his wife in a nursing home even though she may not be conscious enough to know he is there. Every single day. He is not evil, stupid, or immoral. He is a good person whose views differ from mine because he has had different life experiences and pays attention to different sources of information. We need political engagement that acknowledges the humanity and experiences of those who differ with us; that blends the charitable impulse with political impulses, a charitable politics that combines heart and head. At the same time, we should be wary of individuals whose motives and tactics are demonstrably harmful.

Kathy and Jim Win for People with Disabilities

We talk about social justice, and political advocacy or lobbying, and it helps to make a few distinctions. There are many kinds of advocacy. When you write the local newspaper to say that you disagree with an editorial, that is "speaking out to get a result" advocacy.

When a lawyer goes to court to support a client, she is an advocate—arguing on behalf of a client. Social workers are advocates for a client when they help them fill out a form to receive public benefits. Hospitals have patient advocates to help people negotiate the unfamiliar complexities of medical terms and practices.

Rich and middle-class people have advocates, ways of influencing the political process, whereas people who are less fortunate do not have the same kind of access, voice, or funds to get their voices heard. We do political advocacy not just to advance our interests, but also the interests of those who lack a public voice.

Kathy and Jim Rurak agreed to describe a successful campaign to influence policy changes in a program for mentally disabled adults. In their own words:

The winter of 2014 was not only cold. It was cruel. About twenty guardians and caregivers of mentally disabled adults attended a "rollout" of new policies and programs by the Massachusetts Department of Developmental Services (DDS). Clients now working for sub-minimum wages in sheltered workshops would be transitioned to minimum wage jobs in the private sector. Workshop admissions were already closed, and all workshops would be closed by June of 2015.

Silence filled the room and jaws dropped everywhere. Our children loved their workshops and their paychecks. Overall, 48 percent (about 1,200 people) of those receiving services from DDS worked in them. And most of these had tried outside work many times only to lose it again and again.

DDS had concluded that both the segregated environment and sub-minimum pay were issues at the forefront of the next chapter of the civil rights movement. They believed that with the proper staffing, every disabled adult could find and hold a minimum wage job. They had requested an additional $12 million in the fiscal year 2015 budget, and the governor put in for half that amount. Still, they were confident that even with reduced staff, they would meet their goals. They had put in no request to fund workshops.

All the rest of us knew better. Even with full funding, the program would fail. We applauded the effort, but not the ideology. We knew because we had seen it before. Even with the best of staff, several of our dependents would not make it. DDS had no fallback plan for them. If they did not find a minimum wage job for a client, they'd place him or her in what amounted to day-care programs. Many of our dependents who now worked for pay, and were proud of it, would be left in the lurch.

DDS thought it held all the cards. They had already decided their policy (with no input from parents). The governor was on board. Several workshops had been given advance notice and had folded. DDS spokespeople claimed that they were following federal law and that unless they did it quickly, our state would lose federal funds. If we rocked the boat, our dependents would suffer.

But we knew that their ideology and arrogance simply meant a "forced relocation" of our loved ones. So we organized against them. Saul Alinsky said that the "opposition does the organizing." Never has it been so true.

That night we all exchanged contact info and went to work. We divided tasks into research, contacts, outreach, and analysis of the process required to enact DDS's policy. They were weak on all fronts.

One group discovered that there were no federal mandates or laws that required workshop closure. There had been cases, rightly brought, against states where workshops were exploiting disabled workers. But even in those cases the government gave the defendants time to fix the problems and never took away workshops for those who chose them. Our DDS emperor had no clothes.

Another group reached out across the state to other parents with dependents in other workshops. Soon there was a petition with over 600 names demanding that they be reinstated.

Another group had a relationship with the chair of the Ways and Means Committee in the House of State Representatives. We had already concluded that he and not the governor would be the principal author of the budget. He agreed with our case, cut funding for the new initiative, and restored it for the workshops. He welcomed the petition with now over 600 names, and, when the senate version of the budget was more supportive of DDS, he already had gathered support for his/our position.

A key to it was that neither he nor we really wanted to take away funds to support the new employment initiative. We just wanted balance, namely funding for programs that were an appropriate fallback for those for whom outside employment might not work.

In the end, we won. Things are better now. DDS officials are talking to us. They came to realize that without a relationship with their stakeholders, they cannot accomplish something good for everyone. But without our organized effort, they would still be dictating terms, and our children would be the victims.

Neighborhood Organizing, by Patricia E. Myers

Organizing a neighborhood can help build the social fabric of the community, which, along with adequate policing, acts as a deterrent to crime. It is also a way to learn the art of politics and meet interesting people. Our neighborhood wellbeing is in no small part due to the volunteer organizing of several people, one of whom is Pat Myers, a local resident who works tirelessly and effectively for neighborhood betterment. During 2020 pre-election confusion, many in the neighborhood knew that they could turn to her for good advice about procedures for voting.

Pat and I were having lunch at a local restaurant when a plainly dressed middle-aged woman stopped by. They traded comments about grandchildren. It turned out that the woman standing beside our table was a member of the Maryland House of Delegates, the Maryland equivalent to the U.S. House of Representatives. Getting involved locally not only helps meet your neighbors, but can lead to a wider circle of friends, movers, and shakers. Here are excerpts from that interview with Pat.

How did you become a neighborhood organizer?

You don't think of what you get out of it. You want your energies to help people. Some people get involved simply because they do not want to live in a neighborhood that is going downhill and will affect the worth of their home. Everyone was complaining about what was happening in our area, but not doing anything about it. I wanted to turn negative energy into a positive force.

From my teaching and training experience, I have learned that organizing is a gift that is difficult for some and easier for others, much like executive skills. I have been given the gift of organizing.

[She then related several previous jobs that helped build skills and confidence.] You have to be able to identify the best way to put things together to reach your audience and your goal. You must be organized yourself. It is the glue that holds things together.

What are some of the most important steps in organizing?

First, talk with many people and see if there is an interest. If something does not serve a local need and the greater good, give up on that issue and perhaps try another. At my local church, there was some interest in forming a bereavement group, so I did some research, identified trainers, and got six people to agree to participate. But the pastor said "no," so I backed off.

Five years later a woman called and said, "You had a plan for a bereavement group and the pastor is now interested in it." Perhaps it was a better time for him, or he recognized the need or maybe earlier had just not been God's time to start it. I told the caller . . . to go for it and I would help where I'm needed. They went forward, and we had meetings and put a plan together. Since that time, they have been able to support people when loved ones have died.

Describe some of your accomplishments as a local organizer.

I was on the board of the local community group for a long time. The group was falling apart and so was the community. I stepped in and have been leader and active organizer for seventeen years.

Through attending meetings and talking to other leaders, I made important county contacts—where to go with problems, which departments handle which issues, and such. I invited developers, state and county legislators, and department heads to attend our meetings. Half a dozen police department leaders and county and state representatives typically show up at meetings now. We became a strong, respected voice in the northern part of our county.

We walked through the neighborhood with our representative on county council. He was shown code violations and places that needed cleaning up; curbing, and resurfacing needs; the conditions of vacant homes; brush and debris blocking storm drains; broken and raised sidewalks; dangerous street crossings without marked pedestrian crossings.

We educated the community on various issues. People did not know how tax assessments were done or that owners had to sign up to get a tax reduction for homestead credit. People did not know how to go about getting these changes made. We had speakers who educated them. It is also important to empower others. You must give them the tools to be successful. It took time, but because a large part of the community met and showed an interest, others were willing to help or take the lead to address other issues.

For example, we got an approved traffic crossing for a local blind man, a pedestrian crosswalk and sidewalk to access a bus stop; improved trash collections; repaired sidewalks; and we even brought a new program to the local community center. Spear-headed by another resident, we were able to get a fifty-five-year-old unsafe neighborhood park replaced. We stopped the development of some proposed back-to-back townhouses at an inappropriate location and pushed for other needed area changes. When a conundrum arises and the community makes a decision with which you disagree; you have to go with it. You have to go with the majority. It is important to go with what the community wants and not just what you want.

What are some of your meeting strategies?
It's really important to be highly organized when running a meeting. To be concise; to keep to an announced agenda; to keep the meetings moving along. Meetings need to begin and end on time. When people commit to attend a meeting with a starting and finishing time, they expect those times to be met and get restless if you start going over the set time.

I finally found a paradigm that works for our community. Our meetings last only *one* hour. Two or three topics are addressed at each meeting, hoping that at least one topic will interest each person in the community. I set a strict agenda with timeframes. Then I tell the invited speakers how long they have to speak and when they will be speaking. When they near the end of their allotted time, I stand and start moving toward the front. They get the message.

Through the newsletter delivered prior to a meeting and through the listserv, people are aware of the agenda and topics to be addressed. They are invited to submit questions for the speakers. I provide the speakers with the submitted questions ahead of time, so they have an opportunity to secure answers to those questions. Questions may also be submitted the evening of the meeting. The speaker might not have the answers right then but will send an email response later.

The speakers are asked to arrive a half hour ahead of time and stay a half hour after the meeting to meet one on one with people who have individual issues, concerns, and stories. I have found when questions are asked from the floor, they are often not questions, they are stories, their stories. Attendees do not want to spend a night hearing other people's story. They often get discouraged and leave, or they stay and do not come back.

Do not be impolite or personally criticize any of the speakers at the meeting, no matter how much you disagree. You cannot make yourself divisive. And separating friendship from policies and politics is crucial. There are people with whom I disagree on certain policies, but we maintain our friendship.

Try to put responsibility in other people's hands, and don't try to do it all yourself; for example, get them to attend county council meetings or take the lead with specific projects. The more people involved, the better the commitment, the better the community.

As we were leaving the restaurant, I suggested that a nearby road should be widened. The two-lane road, which at either end becomes four lanes, has heavy traffic, especially during rush hours. And since we live in metro Washington where the threat of terrorist attacks and natural disasters can lead to evacuations, a wider road would also provide faster egress in an emergency.

Pat looked at me and said, "See if other people feel that way, and organize to get the change made." It was the perfect answer. If you really want something to happen at any level of government, change happens when you are really committed to act. If you don't do it, who will?

Faith-Based Community Organizing

There are many styles of grassroots organizing. Pat was drawing on many of the same principles used by professional community organizers. Organizers for the Industrial Areas Foundation (IAF) begin with one-on-one interviews to build relationships and determine the interests and commitments of potential allies.

The arts of community-based organizing, or faith-based community organizing, have a successful history of effecting grassroots-based change at the neighborhood and city level. "Faith-based community organizing groups believe that their primary role is to develop participants' leadership skills, build strong networks of relationships grounded in shared values and concerns, and channel those relationships into a civic power capable of making change for the public good."[3] They run tightly scripted public meetings. They are political realists and thoughtful strategists.

The culture of an IAF organization emphasizes mentoring, grassroots education, careful strategizing, political analysis, and public pressure that leads to empowering victories and public accountability. The IAF educates people into the skills and disciplines of citizenship in public life. BUILD, an IAF organization in Baltimore, initiated the living-wage campaign that now reaches cities and towns from coast to coast. IAF organizing efforts are, arguably, the most effective local means of reviving the lost art of citizenship at the local level. They foster citizenship and get tangible results because they practice smart political strategies.

I attended a Washington Interfaith Network (WIN, an IAF affiliate) meeting at a Baptist church in a depressed neighborhood in the

3. Mary Ann Ford Flaherty and Richard L. Wood, *Renewing Congregations: The Contributions of Faith-Based Community Organizing*, UNM Digital Repository, 2002, *https://digitalrepository.unm.edu/cgi/viewcontent.cgi?article=1005&context=soc_fsp*.

District of Columbia. Boarded-up buildings surrounded by tall chain link fences lined the sidewalks.

A thousand clergy and laity gathered to announce and celebrate an agreement for the construction of a new community center, the culmination of months of research, meetings with elected officials, grassroots training, community meetings, and strategizing.

The mayor was there and committed a multi-million-dollar grant toward construction. The archbishop's representative announced that the diocese would donate the land and provide ongoing maintenance for the center. Neighborhood residents also made presentations.

Sometime later, the District of Columbia was debating whether to bring baseball back to the District and how to pay for it. WIN guessed, based on conversations with people in high places, that the council would likely support bringing the Nationals to DC, so to oppose it was probably to lose.

WIN developed a strategic win-win argument. If DC could afford to spend $500 million to bring a team, the city could afford to spend another $500 million on housing in the poorest neighborhoods. WIN's grassroots leaders had done their homework. They met with individual members of the city council and the mayor. They invited the politicos to WIN rallies, where more than a thousand people gathered in churches, typically in low-income neighborhoods. They were disciplined and persistent. They had studied the tax mechanisms that would free money for housing.

A vote was to be taken at the city council meeting. As WIN members—clergy, laity, Whites, Blacks, Hispanics, Asians, males, and females across a wide range of ages and occupations—arrived outside the building, we greeted one another while waiting for the doors to open. IAF grassroots organizations are built on personal relationships. We were quiet, friendly, wore blue T-shirts, and "Put neighborhoods first" caps.

Across the street was a rag tag group of well-meaning young people beating on drums, chanting, and waving "Say no to baseball" signs. They were a small group, compared with the WIN members. They were noisy, disorganized, and ineffective. There was a sharp contrast between people who knew what they were doing and those who had a cause, but not a sophisticated organizing strategy. However, they were showing up to express their concerns and having fun while doing it which counts for something.

WIN filled the council chambers. At a key point, we silently rose to demonstrate that we are watching what the council was doing. When asked to sit back down, we sat. We showed respect for the council's proceedings. We did not need to make a ruckus because WIN members and staff had done their homework ahead of time. Everyone knew what those blue shirts and hats stood for. After weeks of negotiations, the city committed $450 million in improvements in poor communities and we now have the Washington Nationals baseball team.

WIN trains people how to do research, develop political strategies, and learn to speak in public. Participation in IAF is real-life continuing education. People learn while changing the politics of their communities. In politics, you need power to win. You do not build power by losing. Winning strategies and grassroots empowerment are crucial.

At an IAF community meeting, grassroots people who may never have spoken in public before stand at the podium to recommend policies to the mayor and members of the city council sitting on the stage. Meetings begin and end on time. Congregations commit to delivering a certain number of members to participate in a public meeting.

Advance work assures that real policy makers are present, and if they say they will come but do not, a dozen pastors in clerical collars may show up at their office the next morning. For months in advance, people research the issues and the agencies that need to be affected to bring about a change, and they do power analyses to see which individuals need to be influenced to make the change real. If there is a Faith-Based Community Organization in your community, get your congregation involved.

We claim to be a democracy, but democracy is predicated on the *demos*—the people, and thus on their participation. Democracy is about us taking responsibility for our role in shaping local, national, and world affairs:

> "Governments are instituted among Men (sic), deriving their just powers from the consent of the governed."
>
> —The Declaration of Independence

I once asked a college student whether she participated in any social justice or political activities on campus. She replied, wincing, "Well, you know how it is, I am just so busy with classes and friends and cheerleading. I don't seem to have time for anything else." Taken-for-granted dailyness is as dangerous a threat to democracy as overt machinations of those who seek only their own private interests.

The vocation of political spirituality is about how we participate with the power of goodness to overcome apathy, evil, and groups that use their power only in self-interest—goodness in tipping the balance toward good and away from evil on a large scale, the scale on which major cultural and historical battles are won or lost.

Justice is an implication of sociality and experienced at a first level as a sense of what is fair. Gibson Winter describes justice as "the mutuality of shared being that arises from our bonding with one another, from our belonging to one another."[4]

"The Spirit of Goddess Was with Us"

The letter that follows was written during the Cold War at a particular moment in the life of the author. It will sound strange to some readers, even to her now. But it is a vivid example of movement activism as spiritual experience.

> Last Saturday morning I met the Great Peace March at Malcolm X Park where we rallied, clapping and cheering. Then we marched on

---

4. Gibson Winter, *Community and Spiritual Transformation: Religion and Politics in a Communal Age* (New York: Crossroad, 1989), 43.

to the Lincoln Memorial, where we rallied, sang, and danced more. The closing candlelight vigil surrounded the reflecting pool, and the march ended with prayers, chants, and meditations by representative leaders of different religions.

Sunday, I headed over to St. Stephen and the Incarnation Church for nonviolence training. We formed affinity groups for the next morning's protest of nuclear weapons testing at the Department of Energy in DC. There were marchers of every religious and political creed, of every age, from every state and many nations. They are people who have taken a serious look at the priorities in their lives and put nuclear disarmament before jobs, security, nice things, warm houses.

The nonviolence training, scenario planning, and legal briefing went on until 10:30 p.m. My affinity group called itself Divine Obedience. We had an ex-nun, two deaf women, a gardener, a seminary student, George Washington University undergraduates, Great Peace marchers, a married couple, an anarchist, and others. Most of us in the group planned to risk arrest by committing civil disobedience (CD) the next morning. Spirits were high and community intense when we left.

After leaving the church, I had to finish stitching a "Test Peace, Not Bombs" banner. We still didn't finish it up until about 3 a.m. We slept in until 5:35 a.m. and were quickly up and running. At the site, last-minute details, music, and the first few speakers flashed by even as I blinked the sleep out of my eyes. Before I knew it, Arthur Waskow was blowing the ram's horn, calling us to action.

My group linked arms and strode to the main entrance at the lobby. Supporters, media, and police pressed close on all sides. The crush of people swarmed around us as we blocked the sliding doors. It was frightening for a moment because tensions were high. The jostling came close to angered punching and fighting among confused people.

In the doorway, our arms locked together, embracing one another. We began to sing. Microphones and camera lenses pushed up in our faces. Employees of the Department of Energy and police peered out at us through the closed (and now locked?) glass doors. Supporters chanted, "Stop Testing! Stop Testing!" A contingency of Buddhist monks chanted "ohms" and pounded drums in a rhythmic, pulsing chorus. Employees tried to force their way between and through us to no avail.

The original intention of the action was merely to block off the garage entrances where the decision-making and high-up officials park. We wanted symbolically to keep people from getting to work for the morning, to disrupt the everyday, business-as-usual process of testing the most destructive force that has ever been unleashed on the planet.

In fact, we managed to block off every garage entrance, and the 140 doorway entrances of the three DOE buildings, effectively closing down the DOE for about two hours. Our supporters ran messages from one door to the next. The spirit of Goddess was with us all, surrounding us, radiating from us and through us, guiding us, leading us to the roles. Sound crazy? No. We all felt it.

Some of the employees got angry at us and threatened to hit us and throw us to the ground. One man who was really upset called us Nazis. It frightened me that they reacted so strongly to our gentle persistence.

After a few hours in which crowds and media periodically came and went, the police arrested us. They put zip ties like handcuffs on our wrists behind our backs, took our names, and loaded us into the paddy wagon. The crowds which welled up around us cheered, waved peace signs, and threw flowers. My "handcuffs" were loose enough to get my hands out, so once inside the truck I took a flower out of my collar and tossed it to the police and the crowds. It landed at the feet of the police.

We spent the morning in one jail, the afternoon in another. At the latter, all the women who had been arrested at the DOE that morning broke into song. Songs of peace, songs of love, and songs of the strength of sisterhood filled the halls. Inmates joined in. Love was flying around the jail cells, one to another and back again. We shared bologna sandwiches in plastic baggies by sliding them across the cement floor through the bars. The harmonic swells captured us all, and we experienced a community beyond words. These women are my sisters, and the promise for our future.

At 6 p.m. a guard came and released us. The charges were dropped.

Passion, spirituality, solidarity, vision of and action toward a better future for all, not just private spirituality's better feelings for oneself.

People on either side of the political spectrum sometimes experience their cause with the same spiritual intensity as the above. During the 2020 demonstrations triggered by the murder of George Floyd, an Episcopal priest in Lafayette Square said he could feel the spirit moving among the peaceful protesters.

You can view the opposite, demonic spirituality, in Leni Riefenstahl's "Triumph of the Will."[5] Synchronized Nazi marching and drumbeating, youngsters excited to be part of something bigger than themselves, gathered in rows by the thousand, honored that Adolph Hitler is there to speak. "Heil Hitler" salutes. Trumpets blare, banners stream, goose-stepping troops feed patriotic fervor.

They believe that evil will be eradicated, the world saved through fascist politics. If people will just unite around a common goal, make appropriate sacrifices for the common good, the future will be assured, humanity saved. But blood and soil will become soil drenched with blood because violence is at the root of fascist politics. Some political spirituality is irredeemably evil.

Change the values, reduce the heat, add a pinch of theology, a tent, and you have a religious revival. Add some wood, bricks, and mortar, soften the tone, notch up cognition and caring, and you have a congregation. Take away the theology and ramp up the enthusiasm, and you have the excitement of a political rally, a political convention, a coronation, an inauguration. Religion and politics both rotate around

---

5. Search "Hitler Youth Rally Triumph of the Will" and related film clips, e.g. *https://www.youtube.com/watch?v=_hO2NdP5hRc.*

the rituals of political spirituality, for example in ritual references to Almighty God. All-mighty is a power word.

There are legitimate concerns and criticisms of marches, demonstrations, and movement politics. There is a difference between the 1963 March on Washington, which was a culmination of years of activism and organizing, and spontaneous protests that bubble up in response to specific events.[6] The latter may lack institutional structures and clear patterns of leadership, which can lead to endless internal battles and loss of momentum. Governments become immune to many protests, because they know the demonstrators may not have much staying power or political influence.

Passionate participants may be frustrated that the change they want does not happen immediately and drop out or seek even more radical means of expression. Other participants become so inspired by the demonstration's vision and the solidarity of shared participation that they commit themselves to a lifetime of mainstream political involvement. Sometimes a demonstration is a moment, sometimes it leads to a movement.

Since there are constructive and destructive political spiritualities, each effort should be judged by the criterion of the values it articulates and the good it might produce, just as we judge the validity of a theology, congregation, or other activity. Does it contribute to goodness among people and the rest of nature? Does this movement or demonstration aim at, and promote, democracy, liberty, and justice for all, especially for those who suffer most? Is there evidence that this strategy, that policy or group, is more likely to be successful in reaching these aims than some other?

Critics say that demonstrators are engaged in substitutionary social action, in which they could feel they were accomplishing

---

6. Zeynep Tufekci, *Twitter and Tear Gas: The Power and Fragility of Networked Protest* (New Haven: Yale University Press, 2017). Creative commons version available at *https://www.twitterandteargas.org/downloads/twitter-and-tear-gas-by-zeynep-tufekci.pdf*. See Nathan Heller, "Out of Action: Do Protests Work?" *New Yorker*, August 21, 2017, for a review of pros and cons.

something when they really were not—just feeling good without doing good. Demonstrations and political theater are sometimes effective, and sometimes not, just like any other human activity. The George Floyd demonstrations that began in Minneapolis amazingly lit a fire that went worldwide. The March on Washington where King gave his "I Have a Dream" speech achieved lasting cultural significance.

No one knows at the outset whether a particular demonstration or movement will succeed in making the changes participants desire. The cultural kindling must be just right. I have been part of several well-funded, big-name efforts that never got off the ground.

For all that, one Texas woman outraged when her daughter was killed by a drunken driver managed to initiate a movement that gradually led to Mothers Against Drunken Driving, changes in state and national laws, shifts in public consciousness such as the adoption of the notion of a designated driver, and thousands of lives saved. There are many variables and a body of sociological knowledge about what works and what does not.

If you participate in a demonstration or movement, however it turns out in the near or far term, you showed up. You took a stand for peace, justice, and sustainability while others did not. You carried the fire, not just by yourself, and you are not responsible for the extent to which it is successful. That is all we can do. But we need to do at least that much.

"A Suicide Note from Democracy"

> There never was a democracy yet that did not commit suicide.
>
> —John Adams

I came home yesterday and found all my best dreams
stacked like a funeral pyre atop my red and white striped
bedspread. With the white-starred blue pillow shams.
I know they must have been there a long time,
but I had managed to sleep beneath them

without noticing. There was liberty and justice for all
wrapped in a plastic flag on a broken dowel rod; universal suffrage
ripped into confetti in the trash can; freedom of speech
spray-painted with a misdrawn swastika. A hand-written
Preamble against the headboard with words crossed out:
Union, common, general, ourselves, our, United.

How do we forgive ourselves for all we did not become?
For selling our defining demos for a bowl of self-indulgent auto
parts, handguns, prooftexts, and personal privilege?
For never having the courage to face our failures,
admit our arrogance, confront our corruption?
For cheering marching bands of dog whistles and catcalls
in patriotic parades of hate and greed, exclusion and denial?
For leaving the poor behind to sweep up ticker tape,
hot dog wrappers, half-empty cans of Diet Coke, and horse shit?

I never had the will to sew blankets for strangers, cook
chicken stew enough for every pot, or follow my own clear path
toward the common good. Even with map in hand.
For too many years I feared to speak aloud
such holy words as collective, redistribution of wealth,
socialism, economic justice. Instead I sold myself
to the highest bidders, slept with the loudest preachers,
embraced the greediest gropers, and arrived only yesterday
at the stacked-up signs of my own demise—
the bed I had made where I can no longer lie.

I've always imagined this would come slowly,
that I would have time to wrest back control, put on the brakes,
and save myself. But amid the pile of broken dreams
and shattered promises on my bed yesterday,

I saw myself sailing off the cliff and into the rising sea
of history. Already gone. Though my death may remain
undiscovered for decades. There will be no more
perfect union, only this one. And less perfect ones to come.
Justice, tranquility, and blessings will be bought and sold
in free markets where nothing is free and freedom is limited
only by wealth. And what compassion has not yet passed away.

I am dead with no one to blame but myself.
And you, you see me though I am no longer there.
How can I be there and not be there? How can you
still think I live separate from you? Or die?
How dare you imagine us as one and another?
Therein lies our death. I am dead
with no one to blame but myself. And you
who are my self and your own, whose life
is one life, whose death can only be our suicide.

—*Jim Benton*

Part III

Family as Social
Spirituality

CHAPTER 5

We Are Crowdsourced

He knew only that the child was his warrant. He said:
If he is not the word of God, God never spoke.

—*The Road*

Life Is a Spiritual Mystery

Life, in all its parts and whole, is a never-ending source of awe and spiritual experience. No one understands all of life, or even fully understands any part of it, from the atom to the cosmos, from our complex biological functions to human interactions.

We don't even grasp the complexity of our own bodies, composed of ten trillion cells, bacteria that outnumber them ten to one, with an estimated 100 to 1,000 trillion synapses in our brain, and microscopic mites that mate at follicle openings as we sleep and die when they are full of "food" because they don't have an anus. We lose about one million skin cells a day, and the microbes under our right armpits are different than the ones under our left.

If our bodies, let alone emotions and motivations, are mysterious, no wonder we have trouble understanding religious and spiritual experiences. For many of the 55 percent of the world who are monotheists, God is the greatest mystery, more-than, source of meaning, morality, and ultimate power. Other people nonetheless seem to find meaning and act morally.

Sociologist Thomas O'Dea identifies the *limit-situation* as a main element in religious experience. We experience limits but can imagine beyond those limits, and that leads to the desire for connecting to realities beyond (more-than) our limits.[1] Some say that religion

---

1. Thomas F. O'Dea, *The Sociology of Religion*, Foundations of Modern Sociology Series, edited by Alex Inkeles (Englewood Cliffs, NJ: Prentice-Hall, 1966), 14–15. O'Dea

and spirituality rise, in part, from our concern about death—that beyond which we can perceive or comprehend—the eternal soul, resurrection from the dead, reincarnation, unseen forces, unaccountable powers. No one describes this transition more gracefully than Jeffrey Eugenides in *Middlesex*.

> As far as Desdemona was concerned, death was only another kind of emigration. Instead of sailing from Turkey to America, this time she would be traveling from earth to heaven, where Lefty had already gotten his citizenship and had a place waiting.[2]

An eighty-three-year-old woman wrote in response to the Sandy Hook shooting that, given her age, she wouldn't be around long, but that when she got to heaven, she would hug the schoolchildren who had been killed until their parents arrived. We are touched by Desdemona's relaxed confidence and the elderly woman's tender promise.

A few weeks after my mother died, our then-eight-year-old grandson Jasung was in a car passing a cemetery on Thanksgiving Day. He said that at least Great-Grandma was happy now because she could eat turkey with Great-Grandad in the sky. Most of us would like that, and a belief in some sort of afterlife can sometimes help us sustain the difficulties we face here and now, though life after death ultimately remains a mystery.

We experience the cosmos as an awesome mystery: the origin of the universe, the fate of the earth over millennia, the stars, collisions of black holes. But there are also important mysteries in relation to the people right next to us. Spiritual reality comes to us not only from the beyond or from within, but quite fully in interaction with other human beings. Scriptures note the presence of the spirit of God in prophets, kings, sages, and seers. But spiritual reality is present to us on an everyday basis as we interact with family, friends, even the stranger and the foreigner.

---

suggests that religion has six functions: provide support, transcendental relationship, sacralized norms, the prophetic, identity, and maturation.

2. Jeffrey Eugenides, *Middlesex* (New York: Farrar, Straus and Giroux, 2002), 275.

Our world is a *with* world where action is interaction. "Being with is an existential characteristic . . . even when factually no Other is present-at-hand or perceived."[3] Interactive relationships with other people may be the most profound moral, more-than, powerful, meaningful, and thus spiritual experiences in our daily lives, and yet we often take them for granted. Denial of relational sociality is the original sin. Cain kills Abel.

The word "liturgy" comes from the Greek *laós* (people) and *érgon* (work). Liturgy in its first meaning is the work or activity that people do together. The good things we do together are the liturgies of our life in which creativity, goodness, and wholeness can grow. Actions that enhance sociality are spiritual actions.

But decay, evil, and brokenness grow there as well. Jean-Paul Sartre famously wrote, "Hell is other people." Those closest to us sometimes hurt us the most. There was a reported rise in divorces and spouse abuse when families were trapped together during the pandemic. Heaven and hell are sometimes located in the same place. Hemingway said you can criticize bad painters by just refusing to look at their paintings, but criticizing families is different because "families have many ways of being dangerous." Those who ignore us can offend. Those who oppose us may even find pleasure in making us suffer. But hell is also the absence of others.

Spiritual Mystery in Social Encounters

My cousins, Gerald and Edgar, sent a family picture taken in the 1920s. A pretty preteen girl with long wavy hair topped by a big bow looks toward us with a Mona Lisa smile. Thirty years later, I knew her as a gabby cousin.

As she gazes from the family picture, she has no idea whether or whom she will marry. I know. She does not know that she will have a son and grandchildren. I know. She does not know that there will be

---

3. Martin Heidegger, *Being and Time*, trans. John Macquarrie and Edward Robinson (New York: Harper & Row, 1962), 154.

depressions, World War II, genocides, human rights movements, computers, space flight. I know. She does not know that I will photograph her tombstone and place a photo of her tombstone beside her youthful picture on a genealogy website.

She is alive when she stares at me from the picture, though she does not know I will ever exist. She has been in the grave thirty years, bones and dust, when I take the photo. Someday, someone will look at your picture and wonder about the mysteries of your life, your soul, your spirit. Mystery piled behind mystery, hidden by yet other mysteries.

People sometimes express their deep sense of meaning, their spirituality, on their gravestones. In the small North Carolina cemetery where Carole's parents are buried, you can read about what people felt was most important in their lives:

- Guy H. Hyatt, Texas, M Sgt, 4500 Trans, AF, World War II, Korea
- Robert L. Paisley, Lt, US Navy, World War II, Beloved Husband and Father, Senior Dental Officer
- Roy Andre Givles, Sr., "Daddy Democrat"
- Kelsie Mae, Daughter of Eric and Ann Jackson, Feb. 17, 1996, Mar. 18, 1996, Thank you Heavenly Father for sharing your littlest angel

There are embossed images of a piano, an eighteen-wheeler, a Bible, a purple heart, a baseball, a rosary, and the Hulseberg family's large plaque, which says at the bottom, "It's dark in here!" and under it "Shut up Fred!" I would like to have met the Hulsebergs.

The difference between those who bring flowers and those beneath the flowers is the story, soul, or spirit of a particular life. A memorial in the Jewish part of the George Washington Cemetery near our home says, "Nettie: In life you were the force behind life and family. All of us are better human beings for having been a part of you. Life goes on and so will your spirit. You made a difference and are truly missed." We sense Nettie's spirit through words cut in stone.

We each live inside a certain specific set of experiences and memories, a unique biographical narrative, a spiritual bubble that moves along from day to day, intersects with others, and irretrievably disappears in its complex richness when we die.

As Carole and I were leaving the church blocks from the White House after our wedding, a tattered young Appalachian couple with an infant in a stroller emerged through the darkness. The wife appeared to have been prostituting to feed her family. "Please, sir. Could the baby have a balloon?" We gave the child balloons, and they disappeared into the night. Sometimes I wonder about the parents and a baby who now would be about thirty years old if she survived. The mystery of chance encounters of the spirit of the other.

Forty-some years ago, I met two young girls on a mountain road in Sulawesi, Indonesia. One tried to communicate with us. I patted my chest and said "Dick." She smiled, patted her chest, tried to repeat my name, then said "Mnadede," which I took to be her name, though my trilingual friend Marhan Lanting in Jakarta says that she might have been saying "little girl." Sometimes I wonder about Mnadede. Is life working for her? Does she have her own small girls? She reached out. A gift, a mystery of social interaction, a sense of loose connection with the spirit of one of the billions of other people around the globe who are trying to lead good lives— who hope and fear, who laugh and cry, work and play, paint, sing, and tell stories.

While Carole was busy as press officer at the international meeting of the World Federation of Public Health Associations in Beijing, I trundled off to Tiananmen Square. Two young people asked, in English, if I would like to view some student art. A stern Mao-man monitored our conversation from a not-quite-polite distance. I followed them down narrow alleyways, stopped at an unmarked doorway, and increasingly anxious, trekked up steep steps. There, sure enough, was a cluttered display of original art leaning against the stairs, the walls, and hanging from the ceiling of a tiny room.

I bought two scrolls. The art student smiled and said that she had painted one of them. I jested that someday when she was famous, her painting would make me rich. She laughed shyly and led me back to Tiananmen. The scroll hangs in our bedroom, reminding us of the unexpected pleasure of a chance social encounter. I do not know her name and cannot read the signature. By now she might be a famous artist, an agency head, a physicist, or dead. Our lives touched, however slightly, and yet that interaction brings mystery and joy.

The next morning, we looked out the third-floor window of our hotel and saw three dozen people doing tai chi on a flat rooftop. As we walked down a street, we saw a woman doing tai chi all by herself on the sidewalk in front of her row house. In a nearby park, as we started to shadow a tai chi group, an unremarkable middle-aged Chinese woman invited us to join them. We demurred. Our skills were limited, and their routine was somewhat different than the one we were learning.

She asked where we were from, and we said Washington, DC.

"Oh," she said, "I go there twice a year to K Street to work on international trade agreements." Amazing. Seven thousand miles from home, a morning walk in the park and an encounter with a stranger who does trade agreements a dozen miles from our home.

Some people are working on removing land mines. Some are negotiating inter-governmental treaties. Some are caring for AIDS patients. Each in their own way is working to improve the human spirit. The mystery of the human spirit this way passes everywhere, every day.

Back home, as we sit outside a coffee shop, jazz blares from the speakers, rush hour traffic roars by just yards away, a car alarm shrieks, an emergency vehicle screams by—the throb of urban life as the hearts of people rush about, everybody wanting to be somewhere other than where they are. As we sit and sip, we experience an exotic vitality, a Charles Ives symphony of daily public life. Inside the shop, people have come to study at a place where they can be in the company of others rather than home alone—solitude comforted by the presence of strangers, at least before the pandemic.

Who are the people who rush by? What was their day like? Where are they going? What will their evening be like? Are they happy, frustrated, angry? What are they listening to on the radio or cell phone? They are anonymous strangers, yet they have a history, friends, hopes, dreams, vices, and virtues. If you met them in person, they might become your lover, your partner. If they suddenly wheel sharply right, they might accidentally kill you.

But at this moment, accustomed routines prevail, and we get an ever-so-fleeting glimpse of shared spirit of humanity. We may not think of noisy moments as spiritual, but it is here also that goodness, the realm of the spirit of our social life, can flourish if we allow it in. We are mostly blind to goodness when it so casually passes by.

The social world is an incredible diversity of rich spiritual mysteries. The petite Asian woman passing you on the sidewalk might be my friend Jane, a sixty-plus fitness instructor who, if attacked, could jump up and kick a tall assailant in the face.

The young Vincent van Gogh wrote to his brother that he helped some young boys build a sandcastle on the beach. You never know who is next to you on the beach, at the grocery store, on the commuter train. Mysteries of social interaction. Sometimes I offer a silent blessing for the future of a small child walking past.

On the last night of a course I was teaching at The Washington Center, I monitored an exam for a student who had to leave a few days early. As we said goodbye, I asked about her parents who were visiting from Paris. She said they were physicians with Doctors Without Borders, and she had visited refugee camps with them. This I learned in the last minutes of a course on world hunger, poverty, and politics. The student had a lot to teach her professor. A sadly missed opportunity.

While crewing with David Engler in his twenty-seven-foot sailboat from Lunenburg, Nova Scotia, to Portland, Maine, we noticed a blip on the radar about a mile out. The blip continued to head toward our projected course. There was a deep fog, so we could barely see ahead. As the blip approached and showed no sign of veering off, we slowed and steered to starboard.

We waited. Suddenly, a sixty-foot sailboat emerged from the fog under full sail, sailed across in front of us, and disappeared again into the fog on the port side. No one was on deck. They did not expect anyone else to be out there in great ocean spaces and were rigged for automatic sailing. Its was like a ghost ship of pirate tales.

In our daily lives, we sometimes sail in tandem or collide with one another. Mostly we just pass like ghost ships appearing from and disappearing into the mysterious fog of social life. And yet, we are all extended family.

Alone with God

Gurus convene group retreats in forests, beaches, and mountain tops away from the hustle and bustle of the work-a-day world to help us escape from stressful work, roaring traffic, the demands of other individuals, the congestion of crowds. On retreat, we find calm, peace, deeper consciousness through connecting with the Divine and discerning better ways to live. "Alone with God spirituality" can be a helpful, realistic reaction in the face of the overwhelmingly intrusive forces of modern, industrial, commercial, technological life.

But withdrawal and silence are not always good—the silence of loneliness, the death bed, the burglar who sneaks in through the downstairs window left open in summer's heat, of the murderer's hand over the mouth of the victim.

One of the crucial distortions of our cultural understanding of spirituality is the mistaken notion that the best spirituality separates spiritual seekers from the so-called real world—the stereotypical ascetic guru in sackcloth, sitting alone in a cave on an inaccessible mountain top staring trancelike into space and murmuring a murky mantra.

Even the most mystical monastics in the most isolated surroundings seek connection as much as separation, at least an imaginative connection. And even the most insular eremite came to their understanding and location in life through interaction with and learning from others. No human experience—spiritual, temporal, magical, or fictional—exists apart from the context of other humans.

A Vietnamese reporter on National Public Radio says he fears silence. He remembers the war, when silence was the period between mortar blasts, when you held your breath wondering whether the attack was over, or whether the shells were arcing toward the place where you cowered. He says he prefers the bothersome noisiness of urban life to the memories of those silent moments when life hung in the balance. And he reminds us that not all noises are equal. Some are fatal. Others bring joy and new life.

Though we seek happiness and peacefulness in being alone with God, how can we find lasting happiness if we emerge to a world filled with drugs, violence, and poverty? What does it profit us to gain our individual souls if we lose the world? Is it even possible to find personal wholeness and an easy conscience in a world where hunger, racism, human trafficking, and climate change exist? Only if we are numb and numb-er.

No less a spiritual guru than Thomas Merton, who advocated meditation in silence and private settings such as a chapel or a garden, also cautioned against the "perpetual danger of self-deception, narcissism" in privatized spirituality.[4]

In January 1988, my son Thomas and I drove a rental truck more than twenty hours through the night from our Texas home of seventeen years—the place where the children were raised; a place of exuberant laughter, parties, fundraisers, tears, and untellable stories; my community, my home, my sailboat—toward an uncertain future in DC.

Tom helped carry the heavy books and furniture up steep steps to the second floor, then headed for the airport to go back to work.

---

4. Thomas Merton, "The Significance of the Bhagavad Gita," *The Bhagavad Gita as It Is*, tr. and intro. A.C. Bhaktivedanta (New York: Collier Books, 1968), 19.

Travel-weary and anxious to establish a sense some of order, I began to unpack books—Jane Addams to Richard Zaner.

The cedar uprights of the homemade bookcase were too tall for the low ceiling. I stupidly grabbed the circular saw to trim three inches, sat on the floor with the board across my lap, and cut. The board wobbled. I released the trigger and reached to steady the board. The blade ground to a halt in the tip of my thumb. Blood covered the gash. I could not tell whether the thumb was split like an overcooked hot dog or barely nicked.

The wall phone was disconnected. A personal cell phone was fifteen years in the future. The downstairs was vacant. The lights were out next door and might not have opened to a bearded stranger. My doctor was 1,400 miles away. I had no idea where there was a hospital, or even a pay phone. I stanched the blood with a handkerchief and wept lonely, exhausted tears. Yes, I was alone with God. But what I needed was help, a friend, a doctor, even a Band-Aid.

The moment passed. I had not been kicked out of the apartment on that cold January night or forced to stand on street corners selling sex for food as others were. I had not lost my children, country, or future as was happening to others that night. I had not even lost my thumb. If the problem had been a sudden and serious attack of COVID-19, a spiritual meditation would not have provided an ambulance or a ventilator.

Half of all prison suicides are committed by prisoners held in isolation. "The mental pain of solitary confinement is crippling: Brain studies reveal durable impairments and abnormalities in individuals denied social interaction. Plainly put, prisoners, held in cells sometimes smaller than 8 x 12 feet, 23 hrs. a day, often lose their minds."[5]

Our bodies, our souls, other people, our world are all of one relational piece. Though private spirituality thrives in quietude, social

---

5. George F. Will citing Sen. Richard Durbin (D-IL), "The Torture of Solitude," *Washington Post*, February 21, 2013, A17.

and political spirituality are celebrated by noise—the sounds of families on feast days; children at a playground or a pool; the roar of
the crowd at a sports event; the excitement of sharing, singing, and
political strategizing, of committee meetings (well, not all committee meetings) and conventions; the reassurance that others are there
working and playing together to achieve family and public goods,
and that you are joined with them at varying levels in a common will
and purpose.

Our greatest spiritual gifts—our joys, our excitements, our ecsta-
sies, as well as our deepest moments of desperation and despair—
typically come through our interactions with one another. And our
greatest spiritual actions are those which help others. True freedom
is not the absence of others, but the opportunity to bond with and,
where needed, help them.

No Hermits Here

History's hermits seek to escape the rest of us. But they cannot. Ted
Kaczynski, the Unabomber, tried to become self-sufficient and live in
a wilderness cabin with neither running water nor electricity. But he
still came into town for supplies and sent letters with bombs to other
people to attract public attention to his concerns.

While physically alone, his sense of meaning was defined in an
internal dialogue with other people—the enemies whom he tried to
blow up and the public attention it would generate. Ironically, now
that he is in solitary confinement in a maximum-security prison, he is
probably more alone than at any other time in his life. And yet, even
in prison he is dependent on the ministrations of prison staff, distant
electricity-generating plants, and the popular imagination.

We met Christopher McCandless through *Into the Wilderness*,
a book and then movie about his trek into the Alaskan wilderness to
find solitude. He called himself Alexander Supertramp to describe
his itinerant lifestyle. He died alone in an old abandoned bus. But
he had not escaped society. In his journal, he wrote about people

he had enjoyed along the way. On the final page he wrote, "I have had a happy life and thank the Lord. Goodbye and may God bless all!" "Goodbye" and "God bless all" are spoken to the people whom he could not abandon because they lived in his heart and soul, his spiritual core.

Henry David Thoreau, remembered for being mostly alone during his two years, two months, and two days at Walden Pond, began his journal with quotes on aloneness but often wrote about love. He referred to literary classics, to works written by other people, and he wrote letters to other people. It is said that he wanted readers so badly that he initially self-published his journals. He even sent his laundry home to be washed by his mother. So, whether other people were there while he meditated, he was, and we are, continuously constituted by, and in interaction with the social world—past, present, and future. The ongoing spiritual question is, "What are we doing to make it better?"

We Gift One Another

Theologian and geologist Teilhard de Chardin suggested that fire and love are the two greatest discoveries in human history. I would add language, which also comes to us as a product of the social experience of the people who have preceded us, an inheritance from ages of ancestors. Virtually all that we believe and do has its origins in the communicative expression of the larger society of which we are a part.

While the greatest discoverer, inventor, entrepreneur, politician, or author may creatively influence human events, they are still dependent on and subject to the ways of thinking and acting, the language, customs, social norms that originate with other people. And they are powerfully connected to, and dependent on, the rest of us for survival and growth. The dump truck clanking down the road with the "Trust No One" bumper sticker is trusting hundreds of total strangers—people of all races, creeds, political leanings rushing past at sixty miles an hour to stay in their lane.

To get through life, we need food grown, packaged, and sold by other people. We need other people to lay the basics of transportation, the food chain, public entertainment. We need clothing made by other people. We need a clean water supply, furnaces that work, electricity, plumbing, public safety—all provided by other people. Approximately "12.2 million tons of food with a domestic origin (the equivalent weight of 12.2 million small cars) moves into [the] . . . 13 counties in southern New York State, including the five boroughs of New York City" every day.[6] The more than eight million people in that region are dependent every single day on the people who continuously produce, prepare, ship, and distribute that food, as became so vividly obvious during the COVID-19 crisis.

Each of us begins as not-I. We are part of the one who in-bodies us. Physicians and nurses, beneficiaries of decades of medical training from their predecessors, drag us into the first light of day in rooms built by architects, financiers, brick layers, plumbers, electricians, carpenters, and painters; filled with equipment manufactured by technicians elsewhere; accessed by roads built by governments and road crews; in vehicles assembled thousands of miles away from metal, chemicals, parts, and plans; some mined from deep in the earth.

We are cleaned and clothed with fabrics grown and manufactured by workers whom we will never know because they live thousands of miles away. The doctor speaks words in a language that combines a hundred national dialects, gradually standardized by millions of people's usage over centuries. An aide writes down data using a numerical system invented by Arabs thousands of years ago and passed down through the ages by person after person after person. And all we have contributed is to acknowledge that we have arrived. Our spiritual calling is constructively to pass those gifts laterally and forward through

6. Matt Barron et al., *Understanding New York City's Food Supply: Prepared for New York City Mayor's Office of Long-Term Planning and Sustainability* (New York: Columbia University, 2010), 14, available at *https://www.sipa.columbia.edu/academics/capstone-projects/understanding-new-york-city's-food-supply-0*.

individual acts and public policies that promote families, democracy, and a just and sustainable society.

The Blessed Remains of the Dead

The social world makes possible the gift of human life, and then immediately and forever continually showers us with the gifts of the human spirit, manifestations/expressions of a goodness that is spiritual because it expresses the highest values, hopes, and actions of humanity. Literature, the arts (both creative and technical), markets, institutions, and moral and cultural values are gifts that come from the creative energies and hard work of those who precede us. They are there the day before we are born. We did not have to invent them, though we contribute toward reshaping and enlarging them.

We know some of the benefits we have received from the actions of famous people—Lao Tzu, Harriet Tubman, Abraham Lincoln— but what about the seven billion people who are alive today, each doing what they can to survive, thrive, and contribute to our shared wellbeing.

Scan obituaries to read the small and large things that "strangers" have contributed, for example, obituaries (slightly abridged) from a randomly selected issue of the *Washington Post*:

- M, a retired professor in the department of family and community development at the University of Maryland. She had five children, and nine grandchildren.
- K, former *Wall Street Journal* reporter was top spokesman at the Pentagon during the Clinton administration and later became a prominent advocate on behalf of international refugees. He had three children.
- H, a nationally prominent Baptist minister was among the first African American pastors to lead a predominantly White church in Washington, and who helped organize an anti-poverty campaign with Martin Luther King Jr. He had two children, three grandchildren, and four great-grandchildren.

- C, a violin maker who crafted some of the finest instruments of her time, invented new ones, and through science, came as close as anyone ever has to reproducing the venerated sound of the Stradivarius. She had two children and six grandchildren.

- E spent the past twenty-five years at the National Kidney Foundation as assistant to the president and chief executive.

- J, a physicist, specialized in mine warfare and spent most of his career at the Naval Ordnance Laboratory. He had three children, four grandchildren, and a great-grandchild.

- Ca, an assistant to several trade organization executives, including close to twenty years at the Sheet Metal and Air Conditioning Contractors' National Association. She had two children and three grandchildren.

- Jo worked for the Court Services & Offenders Supervision Agency, a federal agency that provides supervision to adults on probation and parole.

- Ke was a roofing estimator. For the last five years, he had been lead estimator for Northeast Contracting, a residential and commercial roofing company.

- N, a retired director of international affairs for the National Oceanic and Atmospheric Administration. In addition to a career of work on weather, he was deeply interested in chrysanthemums. His manicured garden bloomed with scores of chrysanthemum varieties. He had two children, three grandchildren, and a great-grandchild.

- And, ninety-three other women and men—beloved wife-of, husband-of, father-of, mother-of, grandfather-of, grandmother-of, brother-of, sister-of; teachers, soldiers, and a dance band leader, all with hundreds of descendants.

How often have you stopped to wonder about who is helping you by advocating on behalf of international refugees, who is working on mine warfare, who is helping you by supervising adults on probation, who is tending to contractors' associations, who is teaching about family and community development, who is working to break down cultural barriers?

The one hundred and three people listed that day lived their entire lives out of your sight, out of your awareness, and yet each contributed in her or his own way, for better and probably sometimes for worse, to you, me, and the larger society.

We cannot know what or how much their children and grandchildren added to or subtracted from our life together. Who they are and what they do is part of the mystery of life, of our soul-connectedness. But let us assume that, on the balance, they lived decent lives. That alone is a plus if we imagine the effects of destructive lives.

Now consider that approximately 155,000 people in the world die every day, and then imagine the billions of contributions made every single day on behalf of the common good. Goodness persists (intermixed with evil, of course) over time and cultures because we dreamed, struggled, worked, and died to make it happen. It does not just accidentally show up. Our actions, not just our good intentions, made it so.

Whether or not there are ghostly angel-spirits, we are blessed on an everyday basis by those who share our brief time and place in history, who are the mysterious saints and angels, seen and unseen, who affect our lives.

Who taught you to tie your shoes, catch a football, ride a bike, swim, be nice to spiders, enjoy music, mind your manners, remember birthdays?

Who taught you how to read and write? Who writes the news and stories you read and watch? Who came to your wedding and who was supportive for years afterward?

Who taught you how to earn a living, gave you your first job, celebrated with you when you got a raise, comforted you when you were fired, taught you how to grow older with grace?

Who looks after you when you are ill, discouraged? Who will attend your memorial service?

These are some of your saints and angels, the real and visible hands through which we experience the spirit of creativity, goodness, and meaning in an uncertain world. They are large souls who actively bring goodness and connect us with larger wholes. They gave and we got. We also gave and they got. As we join with them, we become co-creators of the transcendent and mysterious spirit of life, goodness, power, and meaning. We are all Mr. Rogers' neighbors.

Paul Harding's Pulitzer-winning novel *tinkers* gives an exquisite description of the complexity of a grandfather clock and the many hands that went into its production. He describes the function of pinions, escape wheels, going train, gathering pallet, mallet, spring, arbor, and escapement.

If we call roll through the years, Huygens, Graham, Harrison, Tompion, Debaufre, Mudge, LeRoy, Kendall, and, most recently, Mr. Arnold, we find a humble and motley, if determined and patient, parade of reasonable souls, all bent at their work tables, filing brass and calibrating gears and sketching ideas until their pencils dissolve into lead dust between their fingers, all to more perfectly trans*form* and trans*late* Universal Energy by perfecting the beat of the escape wheel.[7]

We hear a tick, a tock, notice the pendulum, admire the cabinet. We do not stop to think who and what went into producing this amazing human artifact, an expression of the human spirit, that we so casually pass by.

Early spring, while walking in the neighborhood, Carole and I noticed a stalk growing wild in the dirt between the curb and an ornamental bush that obscured the stalk from the house. As we walked by, day after day, it gradually grew six feet tall and sent out two ears of corn. A bird, resting on a branch, had dropped a random kernel that found good soil and produced two ears with 1,600 more kernels.

---

7. Paul Harding, *tinkers* (New York: Bellevue Literary Press, 2008), 161–62.

We are like that bird. We gather from the fields of people around us and deposit our pickings here and there. Some of the seeds sprout and grow into something alive and nourishing for others. The outcomes spread beyond our capacity to see the full results. The bird has no clue that a seed encased in its poop will sprout and grow. We choose the type of seed, where, and when to drop it. And our actions on behalf of others is a spiritual legacy that joins with the artistic, technological, political, and moral strivings of the human spirit through time to carry the fires of civilization. Sparks from that fire inspire the muse:

You stroll past.

You depend on me
but you do not see us

Our hands hide in concrete slabs
    that touch your feet
    but you do not see us
We hide in your underwear
    Grew the cotton
    Designed the style
    Knit the seams
    Packed
    Shipped and unpacked
    Stacked and sold them to you
    but you do not see us

You think you are singular, self-sufficient
but you are not
We are around you, beside you, in you
We become you and you become us

You speak Thomas Edison's
  "hello," unaware
  it might have been
  Alexander Graham Bell's preferred
  "ahoy"

You think you are self-willing
  but did not choose to exist,
  your color
  gender
  IQ

A fast swimming 0.002-inch sperm
  among 180 million
  met an indifferent egg the size of a strand of hair
  and they said: "let's be you"

We, the many, gift you with
  language
  thoughts
  customs
  values
  hopes
  dreams
  doubts
  peace
  and war

  We sustain your body, mind, and soul
  Without us, you do not exist
You say "I," but your "I" is
the briefly focused "I" of a trillion "we's"

You owe us and others
You are going somewhere important?
Where, and why?
Speak to us.
Ask us what is important
And then act.

"We Are Your Symphony"

In the 1995 movie *Mr. Holland's Opus*, Glenn Holland, played by Richard Dreyfuss, wants to make his mark as a great composer. To pay the rent, he teaches music at John F. Kennedy High School. He finds that he is putting more and more of himself into the students: "Life is what happens to you while you're busy making other plans." By the time he reaches age sixty, the school has decided to terminate the program, so they invite him to lead an orchestra of present and alumni members one last time.

The orchestra members say, "We are your symphony," the symphony you have been writing with your life. Other people and the future are our opus, our *oeuvre*, the symphony we write with our lives as they write for ours. I once heard an eighty-something-year-old, highly respected pastor with decades of service to congregations say, "I've never had the experience of the presence of God. But I have experienced the results in what other people have done."

Jim Benton writes, "A month after my mother's ninety-seventh birthday in 2016, I determined to write a poem and e-mail it to her every day. When she died, in 2017, I collected those poems and others into a single volume. It includes the second poem that she, having opened her first e-mail account at age eighty, wrote back."

"E-Mail Sonnet for My Mother"

I have allowed myself in recent days
to simply wax poetic without thought,
to write what comes in something of a haze
as though whatever object has me caught
is fit for sharing in these daily lines.
And so, I fear, they fall short of my aim.
I've penned these messages as subtle signs
of gratitude and love they fail to name.
Today, instead, I seek to be direct,
to use the sonnet's limits to express
the sentiment I hope you can detect
in other lines that wander and digress.
The bottom line—quite literally today:
I love you Mom. That's what I'm trying to say.

—*Jim Benton*

"A Reply from My Mother"

My Son,
I wish I had words
to tell you
how much I love you.

Thank you
for the beautiful Texas bluebonnets
that you sent
for me to enjoy every day,
along with the priceless poetry
that you share with me.

I like to read
and enjoy your poetry.
I particularly like it
when you share with me
your thoughts.

I think of you,
my Son,
every day
and pray for your happiness.

From your devoted Mom

—*Kathryn Lee Benton Coffey, E-Mails for My Mother
and Other Poems*

CHAPTER 6

Our Souls Overlap

> We recognize our own mortality, and are reminded that in
> the fleeting time we have on this earth, what matters is not
> wealth, or status, or power, or fame but rather, how well we
> have loved, and what small part we have played in better-
> ing the lives of others.
>
> —*President Barack Obama at the memorial service*
> *for the Tucson, Arizona, shooting victims, 2011*

From Me to We

On a day-to-day basis, we experience the world as though we are the
center point, the locus of all experiencing. Up/down, here/there, now/
later are all experienced in relation to our bodies, our consciousness, at
any given instant.

At this moment, I sit in the study at the keyboard with the lingering taste of a chocolate chunk cookie in my mouth. As my fingers
type, my ears hear clicking keys, and my eyes follow letters scrolling
across the screen. If I go upstairs to the kitchen, the kitchen that was
up there a moment ago is now my here, and the study becomes my
past down there.

Sociality (our experience of people), temporality (experience of
time), spatiality (experience of space), and embodiment (experience of
our bodies) shape how we experience the world—me now here experiencing my body, feelings, thoughts, the room, the lighting, the keyboard, the cookie; different than you, later, there, experiencing these
words in a different setting, sans cookie.[1]

---

1. See Alfred Schutz, *The Phenomenology of the Social World,* tr. George Walsh and
Frederick Lehnert (Evanston, IL: Northwestern University Press, 1967); also Schutz's
three-volume *Collected Papers* (The Hague: Martinus Nijhoff).

One of the greatest challenges we have is to balance the over-weening power of me-now-here centeredness with an intellectual and emotional realization that other people are as fully real as we are. For some people, "I want," "I deserve," and "I need" overwhelm the legitimate wants, needs, and opinions of other people. But, their wants-needs-opinions are grounded in their experiences, just as mine are grounded in my experience. It is not always easy to step outside me-feels, me-wants, me-thinks.

As we mature emotionally and realize that the other person is a fully centered self with a distinctive biographical narrative, the possibility of compassion, empathy, and "do unto others as you would have them do unto you" in its many variations across religious traditions arises.

If the other is as fully real as I am, then it is harder for me to wish mishap upon them than it would upon myself. Their time is as important to them as my time is to me; their space as meaningful to them as my space to me; their body as fully sensual to them as mine to me. The religious or political beliefs they hold so very strongly are at least somewhat, if not entirely, dissimilar to the ones that I hold because we have different life experiences. This realization is the ground of a politics that is charitable because it allows for the other person's view as having sources and experiences that are as genuine to them as mine are to me. Not necessarily well-grounded or kind, but, unless they are dissembling or disturbed, real to them.

Families, in the primary sense of the word, are where we (hopefully) learn that other people count. Families are where we begin to develop not only intellectually, but emotionally. If we are lucky, we acquire the ability to love, sympathize, have compassion, and partially transcend our me-only core. We learn that it is an us-world, a with-world. And individual families nest within the larger nexus of the human family, the society and culture that nurture, educate, and sustain us.

We feel the action-spirituality of family life when we hug, cuddle, nurse, celebrate, share, help, nurture, support, and love other people.

"And on That Night, Only People Were Precious"

The word "family" expresses relationships of identity and commitment, at the outset DNA (children) and legal relations (marriage, adoption). However, the Latin *família* included the whole household—servants as well as blood and marriage relationships. Here, we begin with "family" in its primary sense and then use it as a metaphor for the concentric circles of our wider family—local, national, and global.

After spending eight months in Afghanistan, Major J. Mark Jackson made a list of forty-one things he had learned at war, including these three standouts:

- I am capable of performing acts of brutality but don't.
- The Afghan children are absolutely beautiful, with their hopeful smiles.
- Nothing is more important than family. Nothing.[2]

Astronaut Charles Duke left two things important to him when he was on the surface of the moon in 1972—a medal commemorating the twenty-fifth anniversary of the U.S. Air Force, and a picture of his family that was encased in plastic. On the back of the picture of himself, his wife, and two sons, he wrote, "This is the family of astronaut Charlie Duke from planet Earth who landed on the moon on April 20, 1972." The tributes are still there.

When asked what his children and grandchildren had taught him, Stephen Hawking, echoing Albert Einstein, said, "They have taught me that science is not enough. I need the warmth of family life."[3]

In Irène Némirovsky's painful, yet tender *Suite Française*, families in Paris react to the imminent invasion of Nazi troops. They try to jam their most precious possessions in the car.

---

2. J. Mark Jackson, "What I Learned at War," *Washington Post*, May 30, 2010, A17.

3. "Inside a Great Mind," *Parade*, September 12, 2010, 16.

Grab the most valuable things you own in the world and then . . . ! And, on that night, only people—the living and the breathing, the crying and the loving—were precious. Rare was the person who cared about their possessions; everyone wrapped their arms tightly round their wife or child and nothing else mattered; the rest could go up in flames."[4]

If we are lucky enough to be part of a loving family, many of our most profoundly meaningful spiritual experiences are those that occur in the relational activities of giving and receiving. But we do not always recognize these as perhaps the most important source of spiritualty in our lives because interactions are so routine, so mundane. Look around at your loved ones and say to yourself, "This is where the good stuff happens." We are so close to it that we often do not see the spiritual dimension of ordinary, day-to-day relationships.

The next paragraphs were written during a family Christmas celebration in North Carolina. The Blue Ridge Mountains are vaguely visible from the back porch. Children chatter as they play with new colorful new toys. Adults lounge, read, or noisily play board games. The aroma of roasting turkey and baking buns fills the home. A bowl of pickled beets is placed beside my plate because, years before, I had complimented my mother-in-law on her beets. The table blessing seems appropriate because we have so much to be thankful for, regardless of the varied opinions around the table about what sort of God, if any, to whom we pray.

We visit relatives. The aged bedridden brother who will not see another Christmas. His sister, who goes for walks every day and is excited about the imminent arrival of her progeny and their offspring, who will descend into Alzheimer's and no longer recognize any of them. Jobs lost and gained. Money earned and spent. Church fights and blessings. Hugs and "y'all come again soon." Through it all, a spirit of goodness, of family connectedness over generations, of satisfaction

---

4. Irène Némirovsky, *Suite Française*, tr. Sandra Smith (New York: Alfred A. Knopf, 2006), 29.

at making the effort to be kind to one another whatever religious and political differences and distances occupy other days.

The *Hickory (NC) Daily Record* for that day asked, "What is your favorite Christmas memory and why?" Bear in mind that this is Southern Baptist territory, where road signs suggest that all paths should lead you to a Baptist church and from there straight to Jesus, if not in reverse order.

Kim: My first Christmas with my daughter.

Jessica: Going to the beach with a lot of family.

Lea: Getting together with my family at my aunt's house on Christmas Eve.

Karen: Getting together with all of my family at my grand-mother's house.[5]

They did not say church, Christmas music, gifts, baby Jesus, or Santa Claus. They said doing things with family.

Rabbi Danya Ruttenberg wrote in a 2013 *New York Times* blog that friends confess in whispers "that holding a sleeping child felt much more like worship than reading psalms most days." Is there any more spiritual moment than the birth of a child, a wedding, the death of a loved one? These are our primary spiritual experiences, experiences of deep personal meaning and transcendence of self. Love is not just a spiritual feeling. It is a series of actions and interactions that nurture the spirit and contribute to the growth of one another.

"In the Plaza"

Daddy dances
round and round
his daughter rocking round
and round in Daddy's dancing

---

5. *Hickory Daily Record*, December 24, 2010, 1.

love
"Daddy! Daddy! Daddy!"
she declares
round and round the gazebo
pigtails flying in the cool
dry afternoon air
round and round

She waits
with precocious patience
through her older sister's turn
as round and round
her daddy flies his delights
one by one in the plaza
gazebo gleeful
round and
round

Again the younger sister flies
her sleeveless calico hand-me-down
round and round
a bit too long yet
pink socks floppy and soft
in summer white sandals
soaring with lavender laughter
round and round

She dances with her daddy
round and round
flying free
between his radiant smile
and her angel wing sandals

each is the other's delight
round and round
the gazebo they dance
in the afternoon stars
round and round
round and round and round

—*Jim Benton, E-Mails for My Mother and Other Poems*

Social spirituality in its primary meaning has to do with being an agent of salvation in real historical time, bringing life in life to others who are family at-hand and beyond. There is no greater spiritual blessing than to help prevent, where possible, unnecessary death, disease, oppression of people, whether those with whom you live or those whom you will never meet.

We Are All Family

As I walked the Mardi Gras streets of New Orleans with my oldest daughter and her female friends, we saw another group of women across the street walking in the opposite direction. Christi nodded toward them and said, "They're family." She did not know them personally, but they were part of a larger lesbian community with common ties, shared identity, experiences, and meanings.

The spiritual intensity of family groups varies widely from our immediate household to the human family where we are, whether we acknowledge it or not, ultimately bound together as extended family—acknowledged as the primal parents Eve and Adam.

Social scientists suggest that we are wired by nature to connect with one another, that banding together in social groups enabled people more successfully to live and defend themselves. Famed biologist Edward O. Wilson in *The Social Conquest of Earth* points to sports, religion, and politics as examples of people banding together in "tribes" to affirm their identity and challenge other groups. "Everyone, no exception, must have a tribe, an alliance with which to jockey for power and territory, to demonize the enemy, to organize rallies and raise flags."[6]

In *The Seasons on Henry's Farm*, Terra Brockman writes that "An independent-minded bee in winter is a dead bee" because bees huddle together to protect each other and the hive through the cold of winter. If you are outside the huddle, you die.[7] Social groups are our extended family. Our social "huddle" keeps us alive, especially when the going gets tough.

The Jewish mystical philosopher Martin Buber opined, "The *thou* meets me through grace," a spiritual reality. "I become through my relation to the *Thou* . . . all living is meeting."[8] We only become human in the context of other people. As we have no body apart from nature, we have no identity apart from society.

Family Values

In American political discourse, "family values" has been identified with an emphasis on the imagined 1950s nuclear family, against gay rights and other nontraditional pairings. But what exactly are the values typical of real families, however those families are constituted?

Since different families embrace and instill different values, I invite you to pause and make a list of the constructive values that were present as you grew up and compare it with a list of the values you hold in adult relationships today. Then make a list of how you wish to be better at applying those values in your social and political life. In my case it would include the values taught by parents, teachers, church, and the Boy Scouts.

---

6. E.O. Wilson, "Biologist E.O. Wilson on Why Humans, Like Ants, Need a Tribe," *Newsweek*, April 2, 2012, *http://www.newsweek.com/biologist-eo-wilson-why-humans-ants-need-tribe-64005*.

7. Terra Brockman, "The Winter Life of Bees," *Christian Century*, March 6, 2013, 10–11.

8. Martin Buber, *I and Thou*, 2nd ed., tr. Ronald Gregor Smith (New York: Charles Scribner's Sons, 1966), 11, 24.

The Scout Oath:

On my honor, I will do my best

To do my duty to God and my country and to obey the Scout Law;

To help other people at all times;

To keep myself physically strong, mentally awake, and morally straight.

The Law:

A Scout is: trustworthy, loyal, helpful, friendly, courteous, kind, obedient, cheerful, thrifty, brave, clean, and reverent.

In 1942, Lt. Cmdr. John Joseph Shea wrote a letter to his five-year-old son as his ship was about to sail into World War II. His words and deeds capture what he understood to be the values of family life.

Be a good boy and grow up to be a good young man. Study hard when you go to school. Be a leader in everything good in life. . . . Play fair always. Strive to win but if you must lose, lose like a gentleman. . . . Get all the education you can. Stay close to Mother and follow her advice. . . . She knows what is best and will never let you down or lead you away from the right and honorable things in life. . . . With all my love and devotion for Mother and you, Your daddy.

When Lt. Cmdr. Shea's ship was attacked, he leapt forward to put out a fire. There was an explosion, and he was never seen again. His heroic deed reflects the spiritual depth of his words. "Do the right thing," "be honorable," "stay close to family," "trust," "be a leader in everything good," "play fair" are the kind of family values that are needed to undergird a healthy social structure and the possibility of democracy.

Family values enable people to survive and thrive—values like love, trust, honesty, openness, responsibility, forgiveness, fairness, respect, hanging in with one another in good times and bad. If we cannot do that in families, where and how do we think that will happen when the going gets rough with other people? While political spirituality calls for action in the public arena, social spirituality calls for hard work to realize family values in interpersonal and wider social actions. Saving lives is a core family value, no matter whose family it is.

The father in *The Road* seems to be a solitary, driven individual, disconnected from all others except his son. Yet, it was his own social history that inculcated the values, the capacity to love, the spark of courage and hope that enabled him to struggle forward. He does not originate the fire he carries. He does not carry it alone, nor is it his alone to carry. But he doggedly takes responsibility to carry it forward and shares it with his son, who shares it with others.

Though grimly frightening, *The Road* is not only a tale of apocalyptic depravity, but a fragile love story, the most central of family values. The boy is protected by his father and welcomed by another family—"family" because they were accepting, welcoming, and lifesaving.

Heart Friends Help Us Grow

Aristotle wrote that a friend is "a single soul dwelling in two bodies." In the final pages of *For Whom the Bell Tolls*, Robert Jordan has joined a group of guerrillas opposing Spanish fascists in the late 1930s. He falls in love with Maria (Gary Cooper and Ingrid Bergman in the 1943 movie). Fleeing under fire, Jordan's horse tumbles and his leg is caught underneath. "He could feel the snapped-off thigh bone tight against the skin. His leg was lying at an odd angle."

He decides to stay behind with a submachine gun to hold off the advancing troops and give his compatriots a chance to escape.

"*Guapa*," he said to Maria and took hold of her two hands.
"Listen . . . I Go always with thee wherever thou goest. Understand?" . . .
As long as there is one of us there is both of us. . . .
Whichever one there is, is both." . . .
Maria says: "I will stay with thee."

"Nay . . . if thou goest then I go with thee. It is in that way that I go too. . . .

Thou wilt go now for us both."

She argues that it would be easier for her to stay with him and he agrees "It is harder for thee. But I am thee also now. . . . Thou art me too now."

My friend Carl moved back to Texas from Washington, DC after the death of his wife. He met and married Margie. When I was lonely after my former wife left, my children kept my heart warm, but Carl and Margie were the adults who helped sustain me. Other people expressed concern, but Carl and Margie showed up. Let me say that again. They did not just say something supportive, send a card, or email; they showed up. Showing up matters in both our personal and public life.

They often stopped by on Monday evenings, so on Monday afternoons I rushed around the house picking up children's toys, records, trivia; put pots, pans, and dishes in their proper places; vacuumed the living room rug; and cleaned the toilet in the hallway bathroom. Mondays and many weekends we drank, played bridge, laughed, danced, shared jokes and ideas, large and small. Our connection was as a deeply meaningful, spiritual family.

A few years later I was visiting Carl who was in the hospital for diagnostic tests when his doctor entered. "Carl, the tests are back. I am sorry. It is a bad actor. It is pancreatic cancer." Carl knew what that meant. His former wife had died of a long and lingering leukemia, and, before that their 9-year-old son had also died of leukemia.

On a Texas-hot summer afternoon, the three of us decided to sail their blue-and-white twenty-one-foot Venture sailboat on Lake Benbrook. The going was easy in a steady nine-mile-an-hour wind. On a port tack, we settled back on the fiberglass benches, shaded by the sails, and popped open a couple beers, not knowing that this would be the last time he would sail.

"Carl, I've wanted to talk to you about something, but it's awkward. I assume that you have given some thought to suicide if the pain becomes unbearable." Margie was startled, but Carl calmly said "yes," he had thought about it.

"Carl, you know that I would do anything to rid you of the cancer, but there is nothing I can do but promise to be with you from now until the end. This may sound strange, but perhaps I can learn to deal with my own feelings about terminal illness and death by going through this experience with you."

With a crinkly, blue-eyed, Norwegian smile, he said, "Dick, I look upon my cancer as the last opportunity for me to grow, to rise to a challenge." Imagine. You are given a death sentence. But you choose to look at it as a final opportunity for personal growth through the traumas that you know are ahead.

He asked us to help keep him alert, to challenge his mind as he began to deteriorate so that he would continue to be able to make choices. In the meantime: "The sun is shining. I feel relatively well. Let's sail."

Carl was sixty-two when he died a year later. There was a kind of transcendence, a more-than, in our relationship. He and Margie helped empower me; brought vitality, goodness, and grace; helped me learn to live and love more fully; to celebrate life, growth, and relationships. Not just me, but others as well. They were actively involved in hospice, caring for people with terminal illnesses.

Spiritual Identity Communities

In my early days of teaching in seminary, the all-White, all-male faculty gathered for mid-morning coffee and conversation. The chief topic day after day was not, as you might think, the Bible or Kierkegaard, but football or basketball—college, professional, and high school— the players, teams, victories, missed plays, the upcoming high school blue chipper, whatever that is.

Meanwhile, I had visions of social justice and the civil rights movement dancing in my head. The move from Chicago's Hyde Park to Texas at the height of racial tensions and the Vietnam War presented inevitable cultural clashes. In 1935, Jay Berwanger at the University of Chicago won the first Heisman Trophy, but never played for the NFL, foreshadowing the university's decision to drop the sport in 1939 and build the first nuclear reactor on the site of the stadium. Berwanger gave his Heisman to his aunt for a doorstop.

Thirty years later, the university resumed football, but I saw a pick-up game where a counter-cultural student dashed from the sidelines, intercepted a pass, and disappeared down the street with the ball. Since 1960s counter-cultural Chicago was my most recent reality, I was out of touch and unnecessarily disdainful of the Texas football thing.

A social work graduate student, Lon Burnam, who would later serve nine terms in the Texas legislature, started, with others, "First Friday," a monthly gathering of local activists that became a spiritual identity community. The group sustained my faith in the midst of other life-sucking realities—they had a spirituality of engagement that celebrated family, politics, law, and public policy for people, at home and abroad.

These activists found time to participate in human services, legal strategies, and political organizing on behalf of policies that affected the nation's and world's most vulnerable people. They hoped for a better world and had the incredible faith that they could make a difference—the putting-yourself-on-the-line soul-spirituality of a higher calling inspired by the beauty of what-could-be; a spirituality defined by social vision, moral commitment, and practical action.

I was invited to join the Urban Ministries Board. Drug addicts, bikers, and homeless youth wandered in and out of the ratty building. The urban minister, Steve Larson, reported that his van had been strafed by a passing car. And yet when we entered the room where the board met, a feeling of at-homeness swept over me. They were people who shared values, who worked for democracy, the rule of law, peace, and justice; people with a vision about a future in which the hungry would be fed and the neglected respected. Board members sacrificed time and money, and sometimes risked their careers by identifying with marginalized groups. No prestige there. No income there. Just helping people in need.

From an objective perspective, the seminary coffee klatch and the urban ministries board were not so different. Both were rooted in religious traditions. The coffee klatch was a spiritual identity group for the seminary faculty. In Texas, football is an intense, identity-forming social activity filled with religious meaning. "Drop kick me Jesus through the goal posts of life" and its analogs were heard in Protestant pulpits throughout the fall football frenzy. It is a virus that eventually infects virtually everyone, including me. When I came to Bread for the World in the District of Columbia, someone joked that he would make me put on a Cowboys T-shirt and walk through Washington neighborhoods.

Some of the difference between faculty meetings and urban ministries had to do with the way I geared into them; the way my feelings of camaraderie, purpose, and meaning connected with theirs; the way I chose to be present with and open myself up to them—social spirituality.

Any gathering of people who share a deeply felt common experience, vision, and *joie de vivre* are a potential family, a spiritual community joined together in a shared world. Total strangers trapped together during emergencies sometimes hold reunions. Captives sometimes come to identify with those who have abducted them—the Stockholm syndrome. Soldiers who have gone through hell together may develop the strongest bonds of their lives.

Russian novelist Alexander Solzhenitsyn describes the moment when he went from days of isolation in a prison cell to a cell shared with others as "First Cell, First Love." As crazy as it may seem, he says, when you enter that cell that you will share with a random group of prisoners, you become instant family. You "fall in love" with them, he says, out of your need for human contact. Since we do not exist just as isolated individuals, we affirm our essential nature when we bind together in communities. And those communities can sustain and enlarge goodness over time.

In his autobiography, *A Mexican Ulysses,* Jose Vasconcelos describes his connection with his mother as "a spiritual umbilical cord." Human potential is best and maybe only realized in communities. The ways we act a living liturgy in which life, goodness, and meaning flourish or decline depending on what we do, as well as how we feel.

Si Son de Otro Linage

In Camus's *The Stranger,* as a man walks along a beach, he notices that he is being followed. He gets into a fight with one of the fellows and kills him. The fight and murder seem to happen for no reason. He does not know them, had not been angry at them. They are strangers and hadn't done anything to him.

Arrested, he finds an old newspaper clipping on the underside of his jail bunk. It tells the story of a man who left home and prospered over the ensuing twenty-five years. The man decided to take his wife and child to meet his mother and sister, who ran a small hotel. He left his wife and child elsewhere while he "went to stay at his mother's place, booking a room under an assumed name."

> His mother and sister completely failed to recognize him. At dinner that evening he showed them a large sum of money he had on him, and in the course of the night they slaughtered him with a hammer. After taking the money, they flung the body into the river.[9]

We perceive people in degrees of anonymity—from the most intimate to total strangers—which deepens the mystery of connectedness and mutuality. We create epithets to downgrade the humanity of people who are unlike us, especially in times of ethnic conflict and war. They may become loathsome objects to us, not subjects whose lives are essentially like ours, indeed might have been us or our family in the broad accidental economy of who gets born, when, and where.

Who are the strangers? They are the people who are unlike "us," who look different, who have different lifestyles and different ways

---

9. Albert Camus, *The Stranger,* trans. Stuart Gilbert (New York: Random House, Vintage Books, 1946), 99–100.

of living. We too often speak about "the other" without listening to their story.

A Francisco Goya etching, in "The Disasters of War (Los desastres de la Guerra)" series, shows at left a tangled pile of bodies, a hooded person face-down, a child's corpse, and a figure with a poverty-sharpened face and arms outstretched in entreaty to those toward the right. Two women in long dresses, ribbons, and bows look away. The men, in cocked hats, spats, boots, and riding crops, look askance at the ragged locals, and one says, *Si son de otro linage*, "Perhaps they are of another breed (or race)."

An important way to know and get in touch with spiritual reality is to seek out the diversity, complexity, and plurality of the many self-disclosures of the human spirit—not only the beauty and complexity of nature and the cosmos, but also the pluralism exhibited in individuals and societies. If in some sense we are made in the image of God, we can connect with spiritual realities through knowing the Mother Teresas and Martin Luther King Jrs., but also the long-haired, dirty, ragged amputee whose only home is his wheelchair. Spiritual reality (and God, for that matter) has many faces, not just one.

I Still Don't Know His Name

There are those strangers who, if we allow them to be part of our lives, enlarge our humanity and become extended family. During the 1980s, I shared the house with Rob and Colleen, who were smart, talented, committed to social justice, and became family. They were involved in the Sanctuary movement and asked if I would allow a Guatemalan seeking sanctuary to stay at the house. He and others had escaped the violence of Central America and were seeking to educate people in North Texas about the damage that U.S. policies were causing in Guatemala.

It was one thing to stir up things from the comfortable perch of a tenured academic position, and quite another to break the law, so at first I hesitated. "Pedro," as we called him to protect his anonymity, moved in and used the house as a base for political education. He, and others who had crossed the border with him, spoke at churches and any social group that would invite them. Several of us met with our congressman, Jim Wright, who was the Speaker of the U.S. House of Representatives, to discuss immigration, food stamps, a conflict in Southern Africa, and the conflicts in Central America.

I never knew Pedro's real name, though he wrote "Alejandro" on his box of laundry detergent. When he left, he gave me a book on "the untold story of the American coup in Guatemala" and inscribed it,

Para un amigo que comprende y entiende el sufrimiento de nuestro pueblo y lucha para que la pas y justicia sean en el mundo, Pedro.
(For a friend who comprehends and understands the suffering of our community and fights so that peace and justice will be in the world, Pedro.)

We were strangers who shared a vision of how the world could be a better place and a commitment to both the people and politics required to head there. "Pedro," contact me. I would like to know how you are doing, or at least, finally, know your name.

Though he was much younger than I, different ethnicity, family, country, history, experiences, he became extended family because our lives, our sense of mission and solidarity, our souls, our spirits overlapped.

The More "Other," the More We Can Learn

At 3:00 a.m., the phone's insistent jangling jerked me out of bed. "I'm here," the caller said. I had not the slightest idea who "I" was, or for that matter, where "here" was. I will call him "Ken." We had briefly met while I was visiting friends in Indiana. He talked of leaving South Bend. Unemployment was high. Texas looked like a better option, and anyhow he had nothing to lose. He had grown up in a home where eight brothers slept in a single room and four sisters shared their parents' bedroom. Ken, in his mid-twenties, had already spent five years in prison.

Suddenly, this unexpected and possibly dangerous stranger was calling from the bus station seeking help. I brought him home and suggested he sleep on the sofa. He eyed the sofa and said he preferred the floor. He would later explain that my dozen-year-old, child-worn, plush sofa was too good for him to lie on.

I did not sleep well, intensely aware that he was strong, street tough, desperately poor, sexually active, and my teenage daughter was asleep down the hall.

We stood in lines to apply for food stamps and jobs. Initially, he earned money by painting our house, doing chores, and occasional day labor. He shared stories about his life growing up. It was entirely different than my world. In his world, if you saw something setting on the table and you wanted it, it was okay to take it. The person who left it apparently did not need it or they would not have left it there. You clearly needed it, so you helped yourself. No problem.

He was amazed when he received a letter from his mother. "I didn't know she could write." Twenty-four years old and he did not know his mother could write.

His first regular job was cleaning a pizza place at closing. He walked two miles each way, sometimes for just two or three hours of work. He rented an apartment and found a thirty-hour-a-week job bussing tables at a restaurant. Forty hours would have meant that they would have had to pay a higher wage and benefits. When money ran out, he stopped eating until he could earn more.

Ken got a $200 tax refund and used it to buy a car but could not keep up the payments. Good jobs were inaccessible by bus. A car, no matter how old, was his pride, just as cars are symbols for many middle- and upper-class folks. It was also his home, somewhere to live when he could not afford to pay the rent for his two-room apartment.

He eventually earned $80 a week, half of which went to the rent. After a year he quit his job to sign with a construction firm. Winter arrived, and the work became intermittent, then stopped. His car spun out on the ice and was totaled on the guard rail of an expressway cloverleaf. He had no insurance, no way to pay for a tow truck. So he simply walked away, leaving it there on the side of the road. He found bus fare, pulled his few belongings together, and headed back to Indiana. Several years later, he suddenly showed up at the Divinity School. The next day he went downtown to clear up any charges against him for leaving the car and started over. He had dreams of winning the lottery, something, anything that would make the future look different than the past. He urgently wanted to stay out of jail.

Ken's life had not been easy, yet he had a sense of personal integrity and was trustworthy in our relationship. That first Christmas, when I neglected to give him a gift, he gave me a wallet.

When I moved to DC, I sent out a change of address form to 150 acquaintances. It ended with, "Come and see me." Five days later, I received a collect call. Ken explained that he had temporarily moved back in with his mother, asked how I was doing, and promised to come "soon as I can." The genre "form letter" was outside his experience. I was touched that he thought it a personal invitation. I explained that the letter had gone to a lot of people, I did not expect them all to come soon; that he was welcome whenever he could finally make it. I did, however, urge him to call before coming. A week later, a postcard:

> Hay Dick.
>   i got your letter but thing ben up. So you no what i am saying.
> but thing be allright now. how thing going for you? Well Be cool
> and writ back soon in tell everyone I said hi, Ken

Sooner or later, if he survives the perils of inner-city life, he will show up. My Indiana friends had talked him into seeking me out but failed to tell me he might come. But I learned a lot from him—things I did not know that I did not know, as well as things I did not want to know. Spending time with him enlarged and enriched my understanding of humanity, whose expressions are as complex and diverse as the rest of nature. Diversity adds interesting complexity, making our world bigger.

I once asked Sister Tess, who worked tirelessly and selflessly to alleviate poverty and suffering along the Texas-Mexico border, what kept her going. I expected her to say "God," "Jesus," "prayer," or her religious order. Instead, she answered, "The poor. I get my strength from poor people, their incredible strength and beauty." Sr. Tess later became the coordinator of HELP (Healthy Environment Leadership Project), an interfaith environmental justice project at Episcopal Divinity School.[9]

When we lose sight of the "other" as a real human with their own distinctive past and path, we lose part of ourselves as well, because we are essentially one family. We are someone else's "other."

To become more whole, to understand the world you live in better, spend time with people of different races, ethnicities, nationalities, intelligence and income levels, gender, and sexual orientations. And if you claim to see the face or know the heart of God, realize that God is all of these.

Shall We Gather in the Kitchen?

The gurus of private spirituality help us escape from the secular and mundane experiences of everyday kitchen life. But kitchens and congregations are social places where people bond.

In Texas, the house was frequently filled with friends, receptions, fundraisers, and political gatherings. People clustered in the kitchen for conversation, even though the food was spread out on the dining room table and the comfortable seating was in the living room. Members of our house-church gathered in the kitchen to celebrate holidays—leaning on the counters chatting, sitting under the table sipping wine, taking turns in a kitchen chair so the beautician-become-pastor could trim our hair while she danced to the music.

When our adult children arrive for a holiday, we talk in the kitchen, the place where friends and family gather; where arguments

---

9. *https://srsarah.blogspot.com/2014/01/sr-tess-scn-speaking-at-mlk-jr-prayer.html.*

get started, sometimes even settled. There are as many gods in our kitchens as in houses of worship.

It is like the moment reported by Aristotle when some students arrived at the home of Heraclitus, eager to see the great sage and cosmologist. They found him—not on a hilltop gazing at the heavens, but sitting in his kitchen or, perhaps, on the toilet (for there is a philological dispute at this point!). He looked at their disappointed faces, saw that they were about to turn away their eyes, and said, "Come in, don't be afraid. There are gods here too."[10]

In the 1800s, "kitchen" became a metaphor for the place where important political conversations occurred, policy ingredients were added or subtracted, stewed in a pressure cooker, and decisions made. A president's kitchen cabinet is a group of close advisors who are consulted outside the formally designated Cabinet. Harry Truman famously remarked, "If you can't stand the heat, get out of the kitchen." A conservative website says, "Let's examine this giant cockroach (George Soros) that's been running rampant and defiling our 'political kitchen.'"

In 1864, Robert Lowery wrote "Shall We Gather at the River." Today we might sing, "Shall We Gather in the Kitchen to Work for a Candidate," "Shall We Gather in the Kitchen to Plan a Fundraiser," or "Shall We Gather in the Kitchen to Cook Meals for Needy Families."

We Walk with the Wind

Member of Congress and civil rights hero, the late John Lewis described a formative event that happened when he was four years

---

10. Martha C. Nussbaum, "Human Functioning and Social Justice: In Defense of Aristotelian Essentialism," *Political Theory*, May 1992, 213; citing Aristotle, "Parts of Animals," 1.5, 645a5_37. Nussbaum uses this example in several publications, though she doesn't include the toilet in all of them, perhaps playfulness on her part.

old. A terrible thunderstorm came up while he was playing with his cousins. His Aunt Seneva hustled the children inside the house, but "the house was beginning to sway. The wood plank flooring beneath us began to bend. And then, a corner of the room started lifting up." His aunt told the children to line up and hold hands, and walk as a group toward the corner of the room that was rising. The weight of the fifteen children was enough to keep the corner down. But the wind shifted. So, they "walked back in the other direction, as another end of the house began to lift. And so it went, back and forth, fifteen children walking with the wind, holding that trembling house down with the weight of our small bodies."

Lewis commented that through the crises of the civil rights movement, people of conscience never abandoned their moral task. They never ran away from the house. "They stayed, they came together, and they did the best they could, clasping hands and moving toward the corner of the house that was the weakest. . . . And we still do, all of us. You and I. Children holding hands, walking with the wind" in the face of the storm.[11]

We support the other, and they support us and help us transcend ourselves as we pass it forward. Our spiritual task is to learn about and contribute to the well-being of people and the planet though interpersonal and political means, celebrating the spiritual dimensions of our social life, experiencing the goodness that comes through diverse and complex relationships, and actively contributing to greater wholeness in those relationships.

"The Sun Rises Like Fire"

The sun rises like fire
kindled below the night horizon
when earth is darker than sky

---

11. John Lewis with Michael D'Orso, *Walking With the Wind* (New York: Simon & Schuster, 1998), 12–13.

flaming up from the silent embers
of yesterday.

It rises when light is a memory
and hope a wisp of shadow,
beckons us to see anew,
warms our earth again
and calls us to the day.

It rises like consciousness
slowly expanding our sight
'til our blind eyes awake
and open as slowly as sunrise,
as slowly as past becomes present.

When does night become day?
When earth's rotation brings the sun
18 degrees below the dark horizon?
When the solar disk casts 400 lux
illuminance across the indigo sky?

When does the new dawn arrive?
Is it 72 minutes after the Talmud's daybreak?
When the muezzin calls the Fajr prayer?
When the abbey bell tolls for Lauds?
When the Resurrection moment rises again?

When does light birth an infant day?
When you can read without candlelight?
When you can distinguish your field from a neighbor's?
When you can tell if a distant animal
be goat or sheep, if a tree be olive or fig?

No, the dawn comes when the fiery sun
inflames your heart with a vision,
that in each one's face you look upon
you see your friend, sibling, kin. Because
if you cannot see this,
it is still night.

—*Jim Benton* (*based on a rabbinic tale*)

Part IV

Congregations as Social Spirituality

CHAPTER 7

Spirituality with Benefits

Homo sapiens is also Homo religiosus. . . . Theological
ideas come and go, but the quest for meaning continues.[1]

—*Karen Armstrong, winner of the 2008 TED Prize*

Religious congregations are an implicate and expression of our basic social nature. Private spirituality is half-spirituality. Full spirituality is action-spirituality working in solidarity with others to improve the human spirit, most especially of those who are least fortunate. Congregations provide spirituality with benefits—personal support, moral insight, social solidarity, aesthetic satisfaction, a thoughtful worldview, and a link to transcendence.

Congregations, like other nonprofits, also serve as mediating social institutions that help individuals bridge the gap between their personal lives and large financial, political, and cultural institutions. Sometimes, they are the only mediating institutions in town that stand up against the various forces that attempt to dominate our lives, our spirit; though to be fair, sometimes religious organizations also try to dominate.

It is entirely possible to have spiritual experiences outside of organized religion. But it is also possible-to-likely to find fully textured spirituality within a congregation that matches your experience of, and hope for, the human project in the context of a sustainable world. Spirituality in congregations necessarily brings us to a discussion of organized religion, whether the traditional expressions or emergent manifestations of religious sociality.

---

1. Karen Armstrong, "Thinking Again: God," *Foreign Policy*, October 15, 2009, *http:// foreignpolicy.com/2009/10/15/think-again-god/*.

Doubt, Damage, and Decline

Children intertwine the fingers of both hands downward, "Here's the church," raise their index fingers in a pyramid, "and here's the steeple," then they twist hands over to reveal their fingers, "open the door and see all the people." True once upon a time, less true today. It is well known that religious observance has declined sharply. "Southern Baptist churches lost almost 80,000 members from 2016 to 2017 and they have hemorrhaged a whopping one million members since 2003."[2] Thousands of congregations are struggling to survive. Want to buy a church building? loopnet.com/churches-for-sale/ lists more than five hundred at this writing. Probably hundreds more post the COVID-19 pandemic.

Many who traditionally joined a congregation now describe themselves as "no religion" or "nones." More than 25 percent of Americans and Canadians are unaffiliated. The largest number within the American group said they stopped believing in, or rejected, church teachings.[3]

Not surprising. The teachings of one group conflict with the teachings of another even within the same tradition, and both claim to be right. Congregations often focus on the unseen and can claim just about anything. The line between common sense and superstition is dotted, and lane crossover happens all the time.

Some doubters assert that religion is little more than superstition, a relic of the past, and that scientific knowledge and rational beliefs are gradually replacing religious myths and practices. "Nones" may feel they have nothing to gain from affiliation with a congregation, or are afraid that if they attend, they'll be pressured to show up regularly, give money, and do all sorts of things that impinge on personal time.

---

2. Jonathan Merritt, "Southern Baptists Call Off the Culture War," *The Atlantic*, June 16, 2018, *https://www.theatlantic.com/ideas/archive/2018/06/southern-baptists-call-off-the-culture-war/563000/*.

3. Robert P. Jones, "New PRRI/RNS Survey, Almost Four in Ten Young Adults, One-Quarter of All Americans Claim No Religious Affiliation," PRRI, September 22, 2016.

People who are Spiritual But Not Religious (SBNR) retain an interest in spirituality, but not organized religion. Comedian Lenny Bruce said, "Every day, people are straying away from the church and going back to God." Though "spiritual" and "religious" are often used interchangeably, many people think of spirituality as a private search for meaning and personal growth through a variety of psychological and/or mystical practices, are theologically agnostic, and view organized religion negatively. Whereas "religious" typically connoted practices associated with formally organized religion.

It is not entirely either/or. There are many people inside congregations who also see themselves as searchers who yearn for transcendence (more-than) and meaning in their lives and reject or ignore institutionally articulated doctrines but attend for other reasons. "Seventy eight percent of Catholics across all countries surveyed support the use of contraceptives, counter to the official theology of their church, and yet still see themselves as Roman Catholics."[4]

They Sang "Jesus Loves Me" Then Slit the Throat of a Water Buffalo

What it means to be a Christian, a Jew, a Buddhist, a Muslim, a Hindu varies from place to place. There are Theravada and Mahayana Buddhists, Sunni and Shia Muslims, multiple kinds of Baptists. David Nirenberg points out that "scripture continues to generate, not only new interpretations on specific points, but also new scriptural communities and even new religions"—seven types of Judaism, and multiple diverging Christian and Islamic streams.[5]

I was part of a summer Fulbright faculty seminar on the island of Sulawesi, Indonesia. We learned that a public funeral was in progress among the upland Toraja people. We left from Ujung Pandang and

---

4. Michelle Boorstein and Peyton M. Craighill, "Sharp Divides in a Global Poll of Catholics," *Washington Post*, February 9, 2014, A1, A8.

5. David Nirenberg, "Scriptural Conflict, Scriptural Community: Judaism, Christianity, Islam," *Criterion*, Winter 2011, 18–27.

headed north, taking a harrowing bus ride on mountainous roads with curves so sharp that the driver honked lest a vehicle coming from the opposite direction plow headlong into us, yet he could come to a dead stop for a chicken crossing the road.

We arrived in time for the final *sending out of breath* day of a multi-day funeral. The *one whose head is sick* had been dead for the three years it took to assemble the widely scattered family. The Toraja people place a *sleeping* corpse in a casket in a backroom. The casket has a small bamboo tube that drains fluids to the outside. Or they bury the deceased in a temporary grave until the appropriate family can be assembled for the funeral.

Family and friends watched from batik-bedecked bamboo booths surrounding a dirt plaza. A water buffalo, tied to a tree, shifted uneasily side to side over red-stained ground, perhaps anxious about its fate or smelling the blood of its ancestors.

There were speeches in Sa'dan Toraja. A leader rose and spoke, curiously repeating a word that sounded to me like *Jesus*, though that seemed unlikely. Then a choir sang, "Jesus loves me, this I know, for the Bible tells me so"—not in English, but unmistakable to anyone who has done hard time in Sunday school. The Christian missionaries had been here. This was a Christian funeral.

Young men pranced around the water buffalo and pulled its tail. It roared with indignation and fell, but they boosted, tugged, and pushed it upright. A dancing youth waved a large knife in dramatic airy circles, and then with a sudden single swipe sliced the buffalo's throat. Its last, startled, wild-eyed roar turned into a ghostlike rush of air as esophageal cartilage popped free of the neck muscles and lung-breath rushed skyward without passing through vocal cords. The dead man's soul was released to ride his faithful water buffalo, so necessary for survival, to *Puya*, the land of souls. When breath ends, the spirit departs.

The men brought bamboo tubes to catch the blood spurting from the buffalo's severed arteries as its heart continued to pump. The women keened at the departure of their husband, grandfather,

father, cousin, uncle, friend. The buffalo was skinned and cut into large chunks right then and there. Black-clad mourners skewered the stringy meat with bamboo pikes and hefted the pikes onto their shoulders to begin the trek homeward. Everything was shared. The batik banners were stripped from the temporary huts and draped over the casket, topped by a giant Mai-Tai parasol. Men shouldered the funeral bier, moved downhill, waded through a watery rice field, stumbled nearly dropping one end, and climbed the facing hill to a burial crypt. The buffalo's horns would be mounted on the center post of a two-story high-peaked thatched hut along with those of its ancestors.

When is the last time you butchered a bull in your church, synagogue, mosque, or temple? And yet the ceremony was as meaningfully Christian to the people of Tanah Toraja as the funeral of a beloved member with the accompanying potluck meal at the First United Methodist Church in Corsicana, Texas. Both rituals are about death and family, two of the most important realities that humans share.

What sort of God/religion/spirituality do the Christian Toraja people have, and is it important that it is so different from that of Euro-American Christians who might denigrate the animism in a Toraja funeral yet are oblivious to the ways non-Christian cultural themes and memes, such as consumer culture and contrived meritocracy, fold seamlessly into their religious experience?

The Pew Research Center suggests that 63 percent of Jews say their identity is largely about culture or ancestry and only 15 percent say it is about religious belief. The larger culture and religious orthodoxies intertwine and separate in unmeasurable, often subtle ways.

Do Euro-American and Toraja Christians worship the same God? Can it even be said that traditionalist Roman Catholics and snake-handling Protestants worship the same God? People sitting cheek by jowl in a pew have differing understandings (theologies) of who or what God is, as well as what God expects of us. How can there be a single meaning of the word "God," let alone a single understanding or worship of the Being represented by the word?

Religion and spirituality are the way profound human experiences, such as awe and joy, the need for comfort and reassurance, and questions about ultimate origins and meaning are crystallized in explanatory interpretations and reenacted in dramatic rituals. No one knows what organized religion, or anything else, will look like a hundred or a thousand years from now. Judaism and Christianity may be dying though they have proved adaptable. Who can predict how Islam, relatively young at 1,400 years, will change? Will artificial intelligence (AI) eventually experience awe at the mysteries of the universe, become religious, establish AI congregations, honor us as their creator-gods, put us in zoos, or not see a need for us at all? Will unchecked climate change or an asteroid render such questions moot?

Gods, religions, rituals, and songs die when they no longer speak to the human condition. When it comes to religion, like other parts of life, the best we can do is continue to share our experience and knowledge with one another. That sharing is a predicate of our life together, and the only way we eventually find larger and more satisfying truths and appropriate ways to act. Long-term history, our collective human experience, is the practical decider of good and evil, truth and falsehood in religion, as well as in other human endeavors, including science.

Admit the Harm We Have Done

A Gallup poll reports that 37 percent of U.S. Roman Catholics say that the "clergy sexual abuse crisis has them questioning whether to stay."[6] The church's moral and intellectual failings did, and do, provoke my despair and sometimes my anger.

Soon after I began the mission parish in Maine, the March on Washington was announced. My friend Chuck Melchert phoned from his PhD program at Yale and invited me to go along.[7] A member of the

---

6. Michael Boorstein and Sarah Pulliam Bailey, "More U.S. Catholics Ponder Exit from Church," *Washington Post Metro*, March 4, 2019, B1.

7. Chuck later became dean of the Presbyterian School of Christian Education, Richmond, Virginia.

congregational council argued that it would be the biggest race riot in American history. I did not go partly because they did not want me to go and partly because it was outside my frame of reference to do that sort of thing. I have always regretted that decision because Martin Luther King Jr. and the movement were carrying the flames and igniting a bonfire that would sweep through the nation and around the world.

In the 1960s, some religious people marched and sang. Others jeered, terrorized, and beat or killed the demonstrators. It seemed morally clear that God was in the mainstream of the civil rights movement, less clear that God was in those religious establishments that claimed godly, superior, moral, and eternal insight.

In 1963, an African American cook from the Brunswick Naval Air Station, married to a White woman, phoned to ask if it would be okay if they came to our church. When I called on them, it was the first time I was in an interracial home. "Mixed marriages" where I grew up were White Protestants married to White Roman Catholics, aka "papists" whom, we were told, were trying to take over the country.

The council predicted trouble, but reluctantly said they could come. What kind of crazy is that when you must go to a congregational council to get permission to attend worship? What did it say about race, morality, and the state of institutional religion in America? The couple attended for a while.

I began to steep myself in books such as *The Autobiography of Malcolm X*, *Black Like Me*, *Native Son*, *Why We Can't Wait*, *Black Religion*, *Black Power*, *The Wretched of the Earth*, *Another Country*, *Nobody Knows My Name*, and *The Social Teaching of the Black Churches*. I quit giving money to the church and started giving to the NAACP, SNCC, and CORE because it seemed that if God was anywhere, it was in the movement. But then, I was not close enough to the movement to see the sexism, moral failings, and excesses hidden under its inspiring rhetoric and actions. Nor did I sufficiently appreciate what the church had done over the long haul, through the ages. Racism seemed so terribly wrong that, for a time, it seemed to wipe out the good that religious organizations were doing.

We have all heard inane preachers like Reverend Lovejoy of *The Simpsons* or Sinclair Lewis's hypocritical Elmer Gantry. Jonathan Edwards is not the only minister who has preached a hellfire: "The God that holds you over the pit of hell, much as one holds a spider, or some loathsome insect over the fire, abhors you, and is dreadfully provoked . . . you are ten thousand times more abominable in his eyes, than the most hateful venomous serpent is in ours." His intent may have been to praise God who forgives and accepts miserable humans, but it doesn't come off well.[8]

Part of the problem is that we repeatedly hear how great our brand of religion is, how important it is. Yet, Christians and other faith groups have committed holy wars, torture, slavery, and abuse of women, LGBTQ+s, and innocent children in the name of religion. We have sent up the acrid smoke of pogroms and burning heretics, of torch- (and tiki-torch-) lit parades, of burning crosses and treatment of native peoples that obscured whatever flame of love, goodness, and justice organized religion has claimed to promote.

The critics are right when they point out the destructive force that organized religions can wreak. Religion points toward ultimate reality and easily lends itself to fanaticism and horrid acts clothed in self-righteousness, "the word of God," "the will of God."

Pen and ink sketches show Dutch Protestants sewing other Protestants into body bags and throwing them while alive into the river because their victims held "wrong" beliefs. The Roman Catholic record of misdeeds is more obvious because they are more numerous, have been around longer, and—with a rigid hierarchy and ideology—are slow to change. These actions draw our revulsion because they are so profoundly wrong, because religious groups present themselves and their god as holier than thou, though also because we are atavistically drawn to shocking images.

We held religious organizations to a higher standard than schools, families, or governments because churches were so absolute about their

---

8. *http://www.jonathan-edwards.org/Sinners.pdf* (np).

claims to God and goodness. But congregations, after all, were made up of regular people and would only be somewhat (60–80 percent) better than other organizations. We social justice advocates expected religious institutions to take the lead. Sometimes they did, and sometimes they not only brought up the rear, they happily marched against us.

Yet, there were women clergy in the United States before women could vote. There were slave owners who, for religious reasons, freed slaves before the Civil War. There are, of course, still religions that do not permit women to vote or be clergy. The very fact that we expected more from religious institutions is because their public relations effort is bigger than those of Apple, Google, and Microsoft combined. Or, perhaps we had experienced some goodness from a religious institution in the past and were now disappointed that they were not living up to their best selves. Religious institutions present aspirational values, values that point beyond their own capacity to achieve.

In the long term, congregations can be a powerful force for transformative social and political action, and a powerful ally for those who seek to carry the fire and leave behind the guttering candles collapsing on some altars. Jewish, Christian, and Muslim leaders were at the center of the civil rights movement of the 1960s. Jews and Muslims were more heavily involved than the proportion of their membership in the United States.

Training for nonviolence for the Greensboro and Nashville lunch counter sit-ins in the 1960s was conducted by clergy in churches. Many of the Freedom Riders who rode through the south helping integrate segregated communities were educated inside organized religion and motivated by religious values. The movement drew on religious language, texts, and symbols. "We Shall Overcome" is rooted in gospel music and African American spirituals. The movement could not have succeeded without the support of congregations, especially traditionally Black churches.

It sometimes seems as though some critics suggest that organized religion invented torture, murder, war, pain, and suffering. But it was Hitler, Stalin, Pol Pot, and Mao who led to the greatest number of intentional deaths in the twentieth century, though it could be argued that each was in a sense a spiritual/religious movement with a mystical theology, a "Savior" as leader, the promise of more-than, absolute moralities, prescribed ritual methods, and purported racial/ethnic/ national memories.

Even where organized religion has been the oppressor, it isn't always easy to separate the genuinely religious from imperial uses of religion to accomplish political goals, because religion provides a sheltering ideology for beliefs that people are inclined to hold anyhow. The crusades were religious, but also about territory, power, greed, ethnocentrism. Medieval Christians murdered Jews on the way to Constantinople, but then fought one another for control of conquered territory. Meanwhile, most people stayed home and cultivated their gardens.

Al-Qaeda's *jihad* is partly motivated by a conservative reaction to historical forces, especially rapid social change, that is layered with sanction for fanaticism by clerics. While "Islam provides the framework within which ISIS operates," some join ISIS because they hate a rival religious group or are "seeking revenge done to their family," perhaps because of things done "by the American army"; still others join "because doing so offered them an unparalleled chance to rob, rape, and kill"⁹—much like other religious groups at various times and places through history.

Religious institutions would be better off if they reminded their members and the public of the evil that organized religion, including their specific brand, has done as well as the good. The continuous litany of romanticizing God and the religious organization without giving the full picture is an ahistorical, dishonest, and limiting strategy in the long haul.

Official liturgies emphasize individual sin and forgiveness, reducing the need for forgiveness to individual acts. But institutions as well

---

9. Dexter Filkins, "On the Fringes of ISIS," a review of Graeme Wood, *The Way of the Strangers* (New York: Random House, 2019), in *New York Times Book Review*, January 22, 2017, 13.

as individuals can sin and should lament liturgically, ask for public forgiveness, and do public penance when they go astray. More moral and theological humility, less pride. Make modest claims more often and prove godness by goodness, as in "you shall know them by their fruits."

Seventy Percent Is Good Enough

Methodist Bishop James Armstrong said that if pastors felt good about their pastoral position 70 percent (as I recall) of the time, they should hang onto that parish tenaciously. Little in life rises higher than 70 percent satisfaction over time. Loved family may become self-destructive, abusive, and they die. Communities and nations rise and decline. Peace and war, prosperity and poverty, health and pandemics. Even the organs of our body strategize how and when to assassinate us.

Some people say their scriptures or belief systems are 100 percent good. But in the Bible, for example, there is God-sanctioned murder, conquest, sexism, authoritarianism, slavery, and that time it says God killed everyone who was not in the ark. Yet, other people affirm scriptures because they find transcendence and guidance, insight, inspiration, and (variously interpreted) salvation.[10]

Ask, "Is your life likely to be better or worse over time for participating in a congregation? Would your family and citizen spirituality be strengthened or weakened? Does participation in a congregation lead to constructive personal and community support and change or not? What are the values promulgated there?"

Pick the percentage that fits your life when it comes to organized religion. If you believe that religious congregations are, say, 70 to 80 percent better than worse over time (not measured moment-to-moment, the last time worship was boring, or you had a disagreement with someone), consider affiliating with the congregation of your choice.

---

10. For a progressive view of faith, see Sam Gould's *Faith Beyond Mere Belief: What Does Faith Mean in a Post-Modern World* (self-published, 2012), and *Being Christian in the Twenty-First Century* (Eugene, OR: Wipf & Stock, 2017).

Most of us who stay in congregations live somewhere between 60 and 90 percent commitment to congregations. One-hundred-percenters tend to be literalists and fanatics, oblivious to lived reality, contemporary knowledge, and the history of their own faith group, including the origins and meaning of their scriptures. Or, that's where they work. One of Chekhov's characters comments, "I have an uncle, a priest, who is such a believer that, if there's a drought and he goes to the fields to ask for rain, he takes an umbrella and a leather coat so that he won't get wet on the way back."[11]

If you think that congregations within organized religion are worse than better, find some other constructive spiritual affinity group (congregation) like Oasis.[12] Social spirituality is, over time, more powerful and authentically human than individual spirituality because, again, we are, to the core, social beings. Your life is better when lived in concert with others. Surveys suggest that people who participate in congregations live longer.

Even though some of what I hear in many congregations makes little sense, I continue to cast my lot with religious congregations because they do more good than harm and because I do not see other institutions that, day in and day out, century in and century out, celebrate and re-present the central dramas and values of the human experience.

My commitment is aesthetic, existential, moral, and communal, infused by a sense of transcendence—an awareness that reality transcends our moment-to-moment experiences; that we are not alone; that we worship and act in solidarity with religious and religion-grounded moral communities across continents and centuries. Ironically, the very values I have used to question or criticize Christianity were learned in Christian congregations and a family influenced by church and a culture steeped in Jewish and Christian values.

---

11. Anton Chekhov, *The Complete Short Novels*, tr. Richard Pevear and Larissa Volok-shonsky (New York: Alfred A. Knopf, Everyman's Library, 2004), 210.

12. Isaac Anderson, "A Less Lonely Way to Lose Your Faith," *The Atlantic*, September 11, 2016, *https://www.theatlantic.com/politics/archive/2016/09/oasis-secular-groups/499148/*.

Why Do People Attend?

The Pew Religious Landscape Survey found that almost 70 percent of people in the United States say they attend religious services at least a few times a year, with 36 percent saying they attend at least once a week, a self-report that is likely high because people tend to want to look good when asked those sorts of questions.[13]

But many also contribute a lot of money, sing in the choir (which also means a choir rehearsal), count the offering, do the linens, teach classes, lead youth groups, and participate in service and justice activities. They serve on congregational councils, a thankless, often boring and contentious task. They may also cut the grass, sweep the floors, clean the restrooms, and prepare the Sunday bulletins. The religiously observant clearly find value, some sense of meaning in participation.

A Pew Research Center poll where adults could give multiple reasons why they attend services at least once or twice a month cited the following "very" or "somewhat" important reasons for attending religious services:

- 94 percent "To become closer to God"
- 90 percent "So children will have a moral foundation"
- 92 percent "To make me better person"
- 94 percent "For comfort in times of trouble/sorrow"
- 93 percent "I find the sermons valuable"
- 89 percent "To be part of a community of faith"
- 72 percent "To continue family's religious tradition"
- 67 percent "I feel a religious obligation to go"
- 66 percent "To meet new people/socialize"
- 41 percent "To please my family, spouse or partner"[14]

---

13. Pew Research Center, Religion and Public Life, "Attendance at Religious Services," *https://www.pewforum.org/religious-landscape-study/attendance-at-religious-services/* (accessed December 1, 2020).

14. Pew Research Center, Religion and Public Life, "Why Americans Go (and Don't Go) to Religious Services," August 1, 2018, *https://www.pewforum.org/2018/08/01/why-americans-go-to-religious-services/* (accessed December 1, 2020).

Certainly, a sense of a personal relationship (spirituality's *mystery* and *more than*) with a transcendent God is a powerful motivator. But people also go for human reasons—moral guidance, personal comfort, the experience of community and family tradition (these last two an expression of social spirituality). Congregational practice provides benefits.

Religious congregations are an implication of our sociality. We, like many other species, flock together in affinity and interest groups for personal and social benefits, to satisfy our desires and achieve our goals. Private spiritualities have built-in limits because they diminish core parts of the human experience—shared human dramas, moralities, public activities—expressions of our core social spirituality over generations, centuries, and even millennia.

Supportive Communities

Congregations can be frustrating. People who are denied effective power in their work or home lives often express their need for personal power in volunteer settings such as congregations. Successful pastors are often very skilled at interpersonal politics, as African American pastors have shown both in congregations and the public arena.

I once fantasized climbing a telephone pole to cut the wires of a woman who, after meetings, phoned the committee members to undo everything we had accomplished. It was only as people were exiting church on my last Sunday in town that I understood her real issue. She grasped my hand tightly, twisted her face into a childish pout, and though old enough to be my mother, said: "Pastor, I know I've been a bad girl." Literally, her exact words.

Some of her behavior was transference from her deceased father, a strict and overpowering leader in her home church, and not about me at all. Profound human realities and pathologies coexist and overlap in congregations as in other organizations. Religion can bring out the best and the worst—charity and crusades.

Yet, negative experiences were vastly outweighed by privileged moments, such as time spent in the hospital with a thirty-something Bowdoin College professor/husband/father—a leading junior scholar on India, dying of cancer—and presiding at his funeral. Call it "the presence of God" or whatever you want, a deep well of unquenchable goodness can be found in congregations. When a Maryland parishioner said to me, "You saved my life," I must have looked puzzled, because he quickly added, "I mean that literally."

As pastor of a congregation, I formed some lovely, lifelong, extended family relationships. Annette from the Maine congregation's youth group later became an ordained pastor. Her husband David invited me to crew on his sailboat trip from Nova Scotia to Portland, Maine, one of the great adventures of my life. Marion, Ed, and others link with me on social media, visit when passing through town, or remain connected in other ways.

When our 1960s Maine congregation gathered around the altar for communion, the base commander was there, as was the seaman who had just gotten busted back to the lowest possible rank because he had screwed up again. No one ever forgot military rank, but it was put on temporary hold when they kneeled at the same time for communion at the altar. Given the necessarily rigid military rituals, that sort of few-seconds spiritual equality was profoundly meaningful and conveyed a message.

A religious congregation is for many people the most important social subgroup larger than family in which they participate on a regular basis. While family remains central, religious communities can be extended families in which people meet, greet, celebrate, lament, and look out for one another and the larger community.

On a Sunday many years ago, at Luther Place Memorial Church in Washington, DC, we watched five newborns, cradled by parents and sponsors, gather around the baptismal font. Two were howling. Pastor John Steinbruck shouted the liturgy over their scream-gasp-scream contrapuntal duet. The members chuckled, enchanted by the howls of other people's kids. The nostalgia was palpable as we recalled the baptisms and name-giving of our own infants.

Maybe we were thinking about God, but it was the screaming babies that elicited our smiles, dominated our emotional experience, our sense of shared solidarity and historical continuity with total strangers through thousands of years of history who had practiced similar rites of welcoming newborns into the human community—social spirituality. Religious people experience a spiritual presence in shared liturgy, prayers, sacraments, and sermons. But congregations also experience the spirit of life and liveliness in the social context of family and community gathered to celebrate the beauty of new life, the promise of a shared future, and the cries that declare: HERE I AM! I HAVE GAS IN MY STOMACH! I AM THE CENTER OF THE UNIVERSE AND I WILL SCREAM UNTIL YOU PAY ATTENTION!

During a children's sermon, adults might grin at the wiggling and unpredictable comments of the children. Much of the spiritual impact comes from the little girl in her bonnet and bows who blurts out something that throws the pastor off message; from the small boy whose pant legs are eight inches from the floor because that's where his knees are; from the diapered toddler who runs amok down the aisle, oblivious to adult decorum: the sense of innocent, tender, new life in the midst of the gathered community—social spirituality.

John Ylvisaker's hymn, "I Was There to Hear Your Borning Cry" is often sung at the baptism of an infant, though if you look it up on YouTube, it is also sung during secular services or at funerals because it spans a person's life. In order to fully appreciate the hymn, you need to be present to hear the rich lilting melody and harmonies created by diverse decibels and timbres of a congregation as they sing—just as reading the words of Bach's Mass in B Minor is a poor substitute for being in the middle of a chorus full-heartedly singing the opening "Kyrie."[15]

When a congregation sings "I Was There to Hear Your Borning Cry," they are promising to be there with the baby through life's

---

15. There are dozens of videos of the hymn on YouTube, including one by the composer, but most are performance pieces. *https://www.youtube.com/watch?v=WUfLZN-tAtjA* is sung by a choir.

experiences and transitions, and in their dying days. The "I" in "I was there" is God, but also the "I" of the singers, the family, and congregation, a social community, a religious polis, that will be there continuously throughout the infant's life. Some will leave, but others will take their place.

The hymn suggests that we are here to celebrate your arrival in our midst. We will also be here for you in life transitions, sickness, and in health. We will hold your hand as your life ebbs away, be there to celebrate your life and comfort your loved ones after you are gone. We are there for you as you are there for us, as we have been, generation after generation. Though unlovely and disagreeable in so many ways, we are bound together by spiritual bonds.

The current Luther Place pastor, Karen Brau annually leads the congregation outside on a Sunday morning to a small plot where homeless people have been buried. Their names are read, and prayers are offered. What other group walks outside regardless of the weather to recall the names of, and pray for, those who became the least of the least in our social pecking order?

It is striking that though there are always some people in congregations who can be dysfunctional, weird, troublesome, and/or annoying, other people make an extra effort to accept the differences. In other settings, they would likely ignore the problem person, walk away, or quit the group.

Would that our political life had that same kind of acceptance or at least forbearance. Religious congregations are sometimes referred to as fellowships, communities, or family because they provide supportive networks for individuals, families, and strangers, even the odd ones who may be there because they need a sense of community more than others.

Servants under the Radar

It is deeply moving to witness the many quiet and unobtrusive ways members care for and take care of anonymous strangers as well as one another in congregations. It is necessary to look at the ground level to see what is happening. Most of the good that congregations do flies under the radar.

Every Sunday, people bring boxes and cans of food for needy people, not by the tens or twenties or hundreds or thousands, but by the millions and tens of millions—globally through various religions, billions. They give money for charities. They actively participate in community food pantries, clothing drives, fundraising walks.

Congregations host AA, NA, and other support meetings, farmers markets, nursery schools, the arts, and other community groups. Local members encourage the youth, sit at the bedside of people who are sick, and care for people who are dying—not just their own families, but all families because they are motivated by religious compassion.

Congregants participate in Gay Pride parades, rally for women, welcome immigrants, organize demonstrations for peace and justice, buy and distribute school supplies to needy school children, plant butterfly gardens, feed and shelter people who lack homes, make bag lunches for children who do not receive the school lunch program in summer, volunteer in literacy programs, deliver meals to seniors, and raise funds for animal rescue. These activities are carried out quietly and sacrificially, without fanfare or publicity, every single day.

Sure, there are congregations that are anti-LGBTQ+, oppose immigrants, and have beliefs that are dehumanizing. Go find a different congregation.

I am not just splashing Old Spice on a pig (with all due respect to pigs). Look around. Which nongovernmental organizations and volunteers from those organizations provide the most emergency food, and financial and psychological help, 24/7, usually free? Which understand family crisis response to be part of their normal services? Which provide fun subcommunities of social groups, whether sports or dance, that contribute to building the social fabric of society?

Which affinity group has sibling relationships with similar organizations all over the world, including developing countries, that help people think beyond their own tribe and nationality? Which provide space or other forms of support for the arts community? And which do all the above? I would venture to suggest that 90 percent plus of the answers will be "religious congregations."

The Church of St. Francis of Assisi in New York City founded the oldest continuously operating breadline in the United States.[16] There are millions of individuals and groups like these who, motivated by the values and commitments nurtured by organized religion, make large and small sacrifices to help others. The Jewish community has centuries of history in individual caring, social service, justice, and political advocacy, and was integral toward establishing commitment to universal human rights.

Religious communities founded schools, orphanages, and hospitals before governments got around to it and in places governments did not bother to go. They have cared for the oppressed (yes, and been the oppressor—I started with that), the poor, the vulnerable, the immigrant, the sojourner. Congregations have been places of refuge and political sanctuary for centuries.

Congregations make huge contributions to our society. If we eliminated the religious social service agencies and the services provided by congregations and individuals in churches, the social service network in the United States would utterly collapse.

The United Jewish Appeal–Federation of Jewish Philanthropies of New York cares for "People in Need in New York, Israel, and around the world" by:

- Ensuring a safety net for the vulnerable
- Supporting and strengthening inclusive communities
- Encouraging self-sufficiency
- Promoting volunteerism
- Assisting older adults and children at risk
- Advancing marginalized populations in Israel

---

16. Ian Frazier, "Dept. of Kindness: Breadline," *New Yorker*, January 20, 2014, 22–23.

Episcopal Relief & Development, around for seventy-five years, serves three million people annually with programs that prioritize women, children, and climate. In 2018, Episcopal Relief & Development spent $23.5 million, 84 percent of which went for program expenses. In addition, local Episcopal dioceses in the United States have their own charitable programs. For example, "Episcopal Charities provides funding and support for parish-based outreach in the diocese of New York" with a 2018 budget of almost $2 million. And individual congregations have their own charitable efforts in addition to those of the diocese.

Lutheran Services in America (LSA) is one of the largest private health care and human services networks in the country, representing 300 Lutheran nonprofit organizations throughout the United States and the Caribbean:

- Aggregate annual revenues of close to $21 billion
- Serves six million people—1 in 50—in the U.S., each year
- Employs close to 250,000 people
- Engages approximately 150,000 volunteers

LSA is number twenty on the Philanthropy 400, in the company of other charitable organizations such as United Way Worldwide, Harvard University, and the Silicon Valley Community Foundation. It would take a very long list to show all the services offered under the average citizen's, let alone critics', radar.

There are fewer than 200,000 Unitarian Universalists in the United States, yet the Unitarian Social Service Committee has $8 million in income annually. More than 81 million people in the United States identify as Roman Catholic, and Catholic Relief Services (separate from Catholic Charities) has a $1 billion budget and is rated among the top ten charities in the United States.

Though some of the above budget numbers include federal funds administered by religious charities, these numbers do not include the daily charitable activities of the 350,000 religious congregations and individual members, many of whose motivation is religious even though their charitable contributions and volunteer time may go to secular organizations.

"In 1972," wrote a former student, "our house on the Texas Coast flooded. Twice. . . . The second time, my wife and I came down with the flu, and our two small children had no place to go where there was no soggy, molding carpet. My sister and her husband came to our rescue with a place for all to stay, but it was our church that saved us.

"While we were gone, a crew of volunteers showed up, pulled up all the wet carpet and carted it away, swept out the water, and cleaned up waterlogged messes everywhere. Later, a church member well-experienced with such things and with some leverage to apply, met with us and the insurance adjuster. After apologizing for any offensive language he might need to use, he ensured that we were treated fairly and then arranged to have new carpet installed at a price that was within our settlement."

Experiences like this led him to attend seminary and become a minister. "There is no other institution in our society," he wrote, "that could provide that kind of help."

"One Pale Blue Drop, Falling"

1.
We are a pale blue drop,
remembering cloud,
fearing ocean,
falling.

We are each not all,
eden to earth to end,
snowflakes, hailstones, pellets of sleet,
falling.

We are alone and isolated,
fearful of each other,

each of us likewise
falling.

2.

We are slippery drool,
curling from an infant's mouth;
    apple-sweet taste,
    juicy on a grateful chin;
wine dark remnant,
wiped from a chalice;
    dark dose of lead,
    poisoning the poor;
burbling spurt,
hope from a new dug well;
    glistening gems,
    morning light on a spider web;
scornful sputum,
propelled with hate-filled contempt;
    cascades of toil,
    sweat on a worker's brow;
wriggling life spark,
propelled toward expectant ovum;
    final remainder of despair,
    hanging at the end of a junkie's needle;
oozing death stream,
blood from a foot soldier's wound;
    first taste of soupy porridge,
    feeding a starving stranger;
single white trickle of sustenance,
milk from a mother's breast.

3.

Each and all, we know the way
of falling, one after the other,
side by side, before and after,
inescapably alone
together.

Each and all, we know the way
of falling through an unknown time,
gravity between cloud and earth,
fearfully alone
together.

Each and all, we know the way
of pain falling drop by drop,
onto rich and poor, near and far,
despairingly alone together,
and only when we know
your falling is ours
 will justice rain down like rivers,
 mercy pour out like streams,
 and water a world of waiting seeds
 to rise in purposeful acts of love.

—Jim Benton

CHAPTER 8

Congregations Curate, Celebrate, and Communicate the Human Drama

> Suddenly the beach before them appeared shuddering out of the blackness and shuddering again. . . . Far away a faint rumble of thunder muffled in the mirk. I think I saw our tracks, he said.
>
> So we're going the right way.
>
> Yes, The right way.
>
> I'm really cold, Papa.
>
> I know, Pray for lightning.
>
> —*The Road*

Distinguished African American theologian Howard Thurman recalled a day when as a young man he was picking berries in a forest and a thunderstorm suddenly appeared. He realized he was lost. Increasingly surrounded by darkness and crashing thunder, he began to panic. Then he recalled a family saying, "When you're lost, stop and be still, then look around and listen."[1]

So, he stopped and noticed that the lightning strikes created a few seconds visibility. "With each new lightning strike, he walked a few paces forward until he found his way home, guided by the same storm that had frightened him." Regardless of the storms that religious organizations sometimes bring, they also light the way forward, sometimes with flashes of lightning, other times with signal fires on mountaintops.

---

1. Bruce Epperly, "Reflections on the Lectionary," *Christian Century*, October 18, 2011, 21.

Memory and Meaning

Gibson Winter wrote that religion is "the way in which persons and communities understand and live their stories in a confusing and changing world . . . binds persons into communities . . . the way in which temporal beings symbolize and celebrate the whole of the human story that always exceeds their grasp." Religion provides symbol systems that preserve the important memories of individuals and collectivities as we deal with essential themes of the human drama.[2]

Georgetown University theologian John F. Haught says, "I take religion to be the primary way in which people have sought pathways through the severest limits on life . . . the experience of fate, guilt, doubt, and meaninglessness . . . final deliverance from suffering." He describes religion as "anticipation of a rightness that is now mostly out of range," core human experiences, and moral desires.[3]

Atheist Tim Crane says two attitudes describe religion. "First: a sense of the transcendent, of an unseen moral order to the universe, often known as God. Second: an identification with a community that tries to 'make sense of the world' by attempting to bring its members into alignment with this moral order through a tradition of narratives and rituals."[4]

Sociologist Hans Mol, who spent two years as a POW in Germany during World War II but went on to become a highly respected U.S. and Canadian scholar of religion, wrote, "Sacralization can best be defined as practically consisting of (a) objectification (transcendental ordering), (b) commitment (emotional anchoring), (c) ritual (sameness enacting), and (d) myth (dialectical dramatization)."[5]

2. Gibson Winter, *Community and Spiritual Transformation: Religion and Politics in a Communal Age* (New York: Crossroad, 1989), 9.

3. John F. Haught, "Introduction," *The New Cosmic Story: Inside Our Awakening Universe* (New Haven, CT: Yale University Press, 2017).

4. James Ryerson, "What Is Religion? A Philosopher, a Sociologist and a Theologian Give Three Different Answers," *New York Times Book Review*, October 22, 2017, 27. Tim Crane, *The Meaning of Belief: Religion from an Atheist's Point of View* (Cambridge, MA: Harvard University Press, 2017).

5. Hans Mol, *Meaning and Place: An Introduction to the Social Scientific Study of Religion* (New York: Pilgrim Press, 1983), 112.

Religion and spirituality seem to meet a human need and facilitate human functioning. Religions accumulate and disseminate long-held images, messages, commitments, and practices that help people get through their daily lives, and thus religious practice is an important datum to be examined thoughtfully and taken as seriously as we take democracy, which too is an imperfect but important expression of the human spirit.

Congregations celebrate the ultimate mystery of more-than—origins and endings, beauty and chaos, power (muscularity), often attributed to the Divine, social interactions, individual and societal moralities. Organized religion carries and re-presents symbolic memories and mysteries of the human search for meaning across generations and centuries.

As a Congressman and I left the private dining room for members of Congress, he quietly mused that he was a very spiritual person but that he did not believe in church with its rituals and dogmas. I was not about to offend him during a job interview, but gently suggested that whatever else, it takes organized institutional structures to preserve and disseminate memories of the most important human experiences and values over centuries.

Spirituality and religion seek expression in institutional forms. The charismatic leaders become a movement, a sect, and then a denomination.[6] As an institution, it seeks to perpetuate itself and that means socializing the next generation in the faith. Martin Marty suggests:

> . . . all of those people who say they're spiritual but not religious, who encounter the Divine while meditating or at weekend retreats, and who find their "bibles" in the spirituality section at Barnes & Noble are going to start seeking community. . . . As they mature, they'll find that not all wisdom is born within.[7]

---

6. See the argument developed by Max Weber, *The Theory of Social and Economic Organization*, trans. A. M. Henderson and Talcott Parsons (New York; Oxford University Press, 1947); H. H. Gerth and C. Wright Mills, *From Max Weber: Essays in Sociology* (New York: Oxford University Press, 1946).

7. Quoted in "Religion Update: The Road Soon Taken," *Publisher's Weekly*, November 15, 1999. Also, *Context*, January 15, 2000, 3.

Or, in the words of a colleague: "You may decide to raise your own chickens, but many of us depend on organized supply chains for eggs. And if you decide to raise your own chickens, you are still dependent on the success of breeding programs and accumulated knowledge."

An overwhelming number of people in every era have found meaning in religious piety, morality, communities (solidarity), and practices (methods). Some people have experienced martyrdom because of commitments inspired by religion. Moral practices inspired by organized religion influence billions of people daily in often unseen ways.

Years ago my primary care physician told me that she had no interest in religion but since her husband was Jewish, their family celebrated Jewish customs and holidays. As she was doing my annual physical a year later, she confided that she had been strangely moved by their daughter's recent bat mitzvah.

Sometimes religious rituals feel empty, as though they exist for their own sake, and we are bored. Other times we feel uplifted by the rhythms, melodies, language, celebration of important life moments, and awareness that we are joined in solidarity with billions of other people of all races, tongues, stations, around the world, and through time—joined in the mystery and narrative about our collective sense of meaning, best values, fractured lives, and treasured hopes.

People who have no interest in attending formal worship nonetheless may desire quasi-religious rituals at such key transitional life moments as birth, marriage, and death—holy or sacramental elements at the very core of institutional religion. Persons who would not be caught dead in a church invite a "minister," someone who filled out an online application, to preside at their wedding. Well, maybe at life's end they will be caught dead in a church or synagogue. But that is the point.

How many secular weddings have used 1 Corinthians 13:4–8 because it speaks to the beauty of commitment?

Love . . .
bears all things,
believes all things,
hopes all things,
endures all things.
Love never ends.

It is no wonder that people revert to practices with religious overtones, because holy rites grew out of fundamental human social experiences—birth (baptism, christening) as introduction to the human community; coming of age (bar/bat mitzvah, confirmation, *quinceañera*) as transition to adulthood; forgiveness, penance, and reconciliation as making right because we all too often do wrong; marriage as a symbol of important covenantal relationships; holy feasts as symbolic representation of family and community solidarity, an affirmation of our connectedness; prayers, last rites, and funerals as expressions of our finite fragility and hope for a better life, here or somewhere.

What would happen if the central dramas, the most important and best of human experience, were no longer carried forward by religious organizations? Are patriotic or economic structures, symbols. and myths enough? What is there to hold them in check when they go disastrously astray? As a Junior Kiwanian in high school, I learned to appreciate Kiwanis. But few secular affinity groups are going to hold societies accountable.

There may be fewer or more religious people and groups in this place or that, at this time or that. But the religious impulse seems to be as basic to the human condition as the impulse to create, share, and express ourselves in music, drama, dance, poetry, storytelling, and painting.

The world calls out for re-enchantment of the big questions of meaning and purpose in human experience. Religious traditions have been the primary collectors, sorters, preservers, and interpreters of the human struggle for understanding, meaning, and morality that rise out of human experience and are communicated through leaders, texts, and congregations.

Because religious institutions exist over long periods of time, they have the chance to self-correct, however slowly, when they get it wrong. Sometimes the laity lead the clergy and sometimes the reverse. Sometimes emerging cultural insights lead, such as happened with the gay rights movement, and sometimes religious institutions lead directly or indirectly through moral socialization. Whatever the unevenness and ambiguities, it is difficult to find any other institution that could substitute for what religious institutions do.

Moral Socialization

"Bacchus made me do it" was undoubtedly a popular Roman excuse the morning after heavy partying. The spirits or gods were traditionally connected with right and wrong, ritual and moral interactions. Around 550 BCE the *Shujing* records the Mandate of Heaven: "The ways of Heaven are not invariable. On the good-doer it sends down all blessings, and on the evil-doer it sends down all miseries."

Heaven, hell, and reincarnation had a moral and social function. Maybe you had the chance to come back for a second chance to get life right. In other religions, if you were good (or believed the right things, did the right rituals), you went to heaven. If bad, you went to some sort of limbo or hell. And there were religious officials ready to send you there, often self-righteously.

A poll cited in the previous chapter indicated that 69 percent of people who attended religious services said that moral socialization of their children was a reason for their attendance. It is not unusual for adults to drop their children off for moral instruction, but not attend themselves. They recognize the value of religious institutions as major agents of moral socialization of succeeding generations.

Whether a religious group is in the middle of a peace movement or an inquisition, words like peace, justice, kindness, forgiveness, grace, love, and reconciliation continue to be read during worship and in study groups. Words repeated over and over have influence even when we fail to act accordingly.

Religious traditions develop stories, anecdotes, riddles, songs, sayings, and myths that awaken emotions, motivate, and inspire. "People who are guided by different images will be likely to make different decisions and take different actions," shown by the organizations we join or contribute to and, when confronted with a moral choice, the actions we take.[8] Nicholas Kristof writes,

> It may be easy at a New York cocktail party to sniff derisively at a church whose apex is male chauvinist, homophobic and so out of touch that it bars the use of condoms even to curb AIDS. But what about Father Michael Barton [and his work with children in Southern Sudan]? . . . What about Cathy Arata, a nun from New Jersey who spent years working with battered women in Appalachia. Then she moved to El Salvador during the brutal civil war there, putting her life on the line to protect peasants. . . . There's Father Mario Falconi, an Italian priest who refused to leave Rwanda during the genocide and bravely saved 3,000 people from being massacred.[9]

We might add the Rev. Javier Cortes Ochoa, Mexican bishop who is risking his life to stand up against a dangerous drug gang.[10] Or Sue and Hector Badeau, people of modest means, who have adopted and cared for twenty children because they were motivated by the teachings of Jesus which "required them to support the oppressed, to care for the least, and to seek justice."[11]

Religious nonprofits help people express their moral commitments in ways that change structures, policies, and funding. They educate and empower ordinary people to become informed citizens of a

8. Henry B. Clark and Donald E. Miller, "The Role of Images in Moral Decision-Making," photocopy, ND, School of Religion, Los Angeles, University of Southern California.

9. Nicholas D. Kristof, "Who Can Mock This Church?" *New York Times Sunday Opinion*, May 2, 2010, 12.

10. Joshua Partlow, "In a Violent Mexican State, a Bishop Takes on a Cartel," *Washington Post*, December 2, 2013, 1.

11. Larissa MacFarquhar, "The Children of Strangers," *New Yorker*, August 3, 2015. https://www.newyorker.com/magazine/2015/08/03/the-children-of-strangers.

global world, citizens of the global *polis*. And that is a valuable public good. Though there is no good way to quantify it, it is not unreasonable to suggest that the largest organized driving force for charity and justice worldwide has been rooted in varieties of religious experience.

Ethical Guidelines

Ethical guidelines, brief summaries of what humans have learned over time that make society work best, provide starting points for thought, checks against hasty judgment, and can help us make good personal and civic decisions.

Yahweh is described as giving Moses the Ten Commandments to regulate the social life of Israel, though scholars suggest that elements of the Decalogue might have come from Egyptian and/or Hittite sources. The Mahabharata tells the story of a struggle between good and evil; the Ramayana, a journey of virtue to overcome vice. Siddhartha Gautama, the Buddha, abandons palace luxury to find a way to end human suffering after he sees a sick man, a poor man, a beggar, and a corpse. Jesus articulates moral ideals in the sermon on the mount and draws on Leviticus's "Love your neighbor as yourself," a moral injunction shared in various iterations by most of the world's religions.

> Hinduism: Do not unto others that which if done to you would cause pain. —*Mahabharata 5:1517*
>
> Islam: Not one of you truly believes until you wish for others what you wish for yourself. —*Prophet Muhammad, Hadith*
>
> Buddhism: Treat not others in ways that you yourself would find hurtful. —*Buddha, Udanavarga 5:18*
>
> Taoism: To those who are good to me I am good, and to those who are not good to me, I am also good.
>
> Zoroastrianism: Whatever you do not approve of for yourself, do not approve for anyone else.

Sikhism: I am a stranger to no one; and no one is a stranger to me. Indeed, I am a friend to all. —*Guru Granth Sahib, p. 1299*

Jainism: One should treat all creatures in the world as one would like to be treated. —*Mahavira, Sutrakritanga*

Baha'i: Lay not on any soul a load that you would not wish to be laid upon you. —*Baha'u'llah, Gleanings*

Confucianism: What you do not want done to yourself, do not do unto others. —*Confucius, Analects 15:23*

"Sufism began as a pious reaction against the growing worldliness of Muslims . . . and rich people, who were likely to be corrupted by their power and wealth."[12] During Ramadan, Muslims are enjoined to pray more regularly, spend more time socializing with friends and family, and do additional good deeds. "Islam will always stand for justice and any path that is taken towards justice is bound to be in harmony with the *Shrai ah* and can never be against it."[13]

While in Indonesia at Gadjah Mada University in Yogyakarta, we learned about Pancasila, the five principles that form the philosophy of the Indonesian state—belief that one god underlies Indonesia's many religions, just and civilized humanity, social justice, democracy, and the unity of the many peoples of Indonesia. Pancasila is taught in schools and is particularly interesting because it is state sponsored. The nation has official standards that are both religious and ethical guidelines.

At Gadja Mada, a woman lecturing on the Muslim faith began, "The central tenet of the Muslim faith is morality." I wanted to jump up and say: "Where do I join?" Of course, when it comes to specifics, there are disagreements about what morality requires, as suggested by her head scarf. But there are also disagreements about moral behavior in my own tradition. When the national denomination voted to

---

12. Valerie J. Hoffman, "Eating and Fasting for God in Sufi Tradition," *Journal of the American Academy of Religion,* Fall 1995, 469.

13. Qayyim al-Jawziyyah (1350), quoted in Mohammad Hashim Kamali, *Freedom, Equality and Justice in Islam* (Kuala Lumpur: Islamic Texts Society, 2002), xi.

support the LGBTQ community, the congregation in which I grew up left the denomination "for biblical reasons."

Religious communities, like other human groups, seek ways to explain and regulate their internal and external lives—specific rituals, sacred places, sacred times, and guidelines for personal holiness or sanctification. A devotee approaches a sacred place or observes a sacred time in a ritually prescribed manner. Rituals with their right way and wrong way of doing things reinforce notions that there are right and wrong ways of acting, and "right and wrong" easily transform into ethical guides.

In ancient texts and present practice, religious organizations offer a teaching magisterium of moral guidelines, a carefully considered, highly articulated body of moral guidance accumulated over time. The existence of religious moral codes provides a source against which we can compare our own practices with the received wisdom of previous eras; wisdom accumulated and continuously tested across cultures and generations, typically maintained and preserved by religious traditions.

Moral codes can become ossified and dysfunctional over time. But they remain a valuable resource if we also take into account real situations, empirical evidence, and contemporary understanding.

When the bishops of the U.S. Catholic Conference issue a policy statement on an issue such as peace or economic life, we can all benefit from wrestling with what they say. Whether we agree or disagree with the details, their ethical insight enriches public conversation. The following is an abridged summary of lists of Roman Catholic social teachings.

- The dignity of individuals and, collectively, as society.
- Family, community, and participation. "Everyone has a responsibility to contribute to the good of the whole society, to the common good."
- Option for the poor and vulnerable. The moral test of a society is how it treats its most vulnerable members.

- Rights balanced with responsibilities.
- Role of government and subsidiarity. "Functions of government should be performed at the lowest level possible, as long as they can be performed adequately."
- The dignity of work and the rights of workers. "The economy must serve people, not the other way around."
- Care for, stewardship of, God's Creation.
- Global solidarity. "We are one human family. . . . Loving our neighbor has global dimensions in a shrinking world. At the core of the virtue of solidarity is the pursuit of justice and peace."[14]

Though moral guides can be helpful, they sometimes conflict with one another when you get down to specific cases. "Principles . . . fail to capture the fine detail of the concrete particular, which is the subject matter of ethical choice. This must be seized in a confrontation with the situation itself. . . ."[15]

The past-president of the Society of Christian Ethics, Miguel A. De La Torre, says, "The underlying problem with Eurocentric ethics is that moral reasoning is done from the realm of abstractions." He argues for an ethics rooted in the particularities of human experience and actions as a healthy corrective.[16] Begin with real people in real settings. They know where they hurt. Whether you start with general principles or actual situations, both are essential to serious moral reflection.

---

14. Catholic Charities of St. Paul and Minneapolis, "Catholic Social Teaching." *https://www.cctwincities.org/education-advocacy/catholic-social-teaching/*. Thomas Massaro, S.J., *Living Justice: Catholic Social Teaching in Action* (Lanham, MD: Sheed & Ward, 2000), chapter 5. See also United States Conference of Catholic Bishops, and "Forming Consciences for Faithful Citizenship," USCCB, *http://www.usccb.org/issues-and-action/faithful-citizenship/upload/forming-consciences-for-faithful-citizenship.pdf.*

15. Martha C. Nussbaum, *The Fragility of Goodness*, second edition (Cambridge: Cambridge University Press, 2001), 300–01.

16. Miguel A. De La Torre, "Doing Latina/o Ethics from the Margins of Empire: Liberating the Colonized Mind," *Journal of the Society of Christian Ethics*, Spring/Summer 2013, 8.

Non-religious people also turn to religious sources, models, and guidelines during life transitions, in times of personal or social crisis, or to seek guidance about how life should be lived. "Most people, when they face crucial moral and ethical questions, somehow . . . have religious outlooks in the front or back of their minds that often sail under the label 'secular rationality.'"[17]

Anyone closely familiar with religious institutions can name women and men whose activism on behalf of other people and nature, like mine, was grounded in moral socialization of religious institutions, even people who no longer attend. Many of the people whom I interviewed for *Up From Apathy* had received moral formation in religious institutions, though they were no longer observant.

A Place to Celebrate Life with Others

Katherine Kinkade, the founder of a Utopian commune, learned hymn-singing in a fundamentalist high school, and though she later became an atheist, she continued to attend a congregation because she found joy in singing. The Grace Chorale of Brooklyn catches the spirit of many congregations in their pandemic online virtual, "How Can I Keep from Singing."[18]

James Baldwin wrote, "There is no music like that (church) music, no drama like the saints rejoicing, the sinners moaning, the tambourines racing, and all those voices coming together and crying holy unto the Lord."[19]

Music is a key ingredient in the fresh wave of nontheistic congregations and community groups, such as the spiritual chanting of kirtans and the community sing-a-longs at the Levine School of Music in

17. martin e MARTY, "Ethics in the Real World: Giving Religion a Voice," *The Park Ridge Center Bulletin,* July/August 2001, 15.

18. NYC Virtual Choir and Orchestra, "How Can I Keep from Singing," YouTube, May 9, 2020, *https://www.youtube.com/watch?v=VLPP3XmYxXg.*

19. James Baldwin, "Letter from a Region in my Mind," November 17, 1962, reprinted in *New Yorker,* December 3, 2018, *https://www.newyorker.com/magazine/1962/11/17/letter-from-a-region-in-my-mind.*

DC and *Choir! Choir! Choir!* that my friend Melissa attended weekly in Toronto. Prisoners in World War II concentration camps played and composed music. One man used charcoal given for diarrhea to write scores on toilet paper. Some of the songs I sing in church have been sung by generations of my family.

My daughter Karen and her husband Craig's then-five-year-old Rosalind once referred to a minister as the "halleluiah man," because he led the congregation singing the hallelujah. Where else but in a congregation will you hear the rhythmic shifts of a choir sliding in a single breath from the Latin chant "In Paradisum Deducant te Angeli" to the South African "Ipharadisi Ikhaya Labafile," as I once heard at Luther Place in DC?

Religious congregations are public places where you with others in your community come to listen, teach, bond, pray, and sing. Where else can you go every week to sing as loud as you can with others, and if you are lucky, to hear great music? (On the other hand, radio comedian Fred Allen supposedly said, "The first time I sang in the church choir, two hundred people changed their religion.")

I am using "sing" both literally and metaphorically for the various expressive and aesthetic experiences that are part of congregational life. In Greek mythology, Mnemosyne (memory) was the mother of the nine Muses, including poetry, music, history, tragedy, hymns, and dance. The arts are siblings of religious experience.

It is no accident that religious institutions, with their imaginative visions of beginnings before beginnings, better mid-courses, and endings beyond endings, have been sponsors of and are filled with creative and inspirational art, architecture, and music. Religious rituals are dramatic, aesthetic reproductions of core human experiences.

The arts disclose, intensify, and disrupt human experience. They track creative continuities and discontinuities in human social and historical life. They stimulate the imagination and, in drawing attention to order and disorder in the human condition, have moral implications. Astute dictators know that to control a people you must put boundaries on both extant religion and the arts, or create state versions, because the arts and religion are siblings.

Religious communities project visions of perfection—past or future, the age that once was and/or the hope for an eschatological future, "a new heaven and earth." These visions have aesthetic as well as moral dimensions. Any time you generate notions of a perfect world, that perfection becomes an inspiration and partial template for life today.

Congregations and Politics

People say that religion and politics are the two subjects to avoid at family gatherings and congregations because they easily lead to anger and alienation. Religion and politics can have such a strong emotional claim that combining the two can be perilous to social relations.

When a national government claims grounding in religion, or when a religious organization can enforce its views through the power of the state, neither is tenable. Many of religion's worst sins have been when they had the political power to enforce their views. And many of politics' worst sins have been when governments have claimed religious or quasi-religious warrant.

No form of human association is so free of ambiguity and the potential for error that it should claim to be a ruling manifestation of the will of the Divine, especially national governments because they have the power of police and military to enforce their decisions. It is possible to start a revolution against a state, to argue with a philosopher, to join a different temple, but how do you argue against the will of God? Unfortunately, when political figures invoke God, it is often just a convenient rhetorical strategy to gain political support, whether through piety or authority.

There are many instances where religion has aligned itself with rich and powerful people, who control, or strongly influence, governments. Mexican revolutionary general Pancho Villá wrote, "Remember Sr. Priest, that our Revolution is the struggle of the poor against the rich, who thrive on the poverty of the poor. . . . our justice involves such holiness that the priests and the churches who deny us their help have forfeited their claim to be men of God."[20]

On September 16, 1810, in Dolores, Mexico, Father Miguel Hidalgo y Costilla preached a sermon (*El Grito de Dolores*) about policies toward poor people. Following the service, he and some parishioners charged out of the church—a "motley band of poorly armed Indians and mestizos . . . picking up hundreds of recruits along the way" and started a revolution. *El Dies y Seis de Septiembre* is celebrated as Mexican Independence Day and Hidalgo as the father of Mexican independence.

Some clergy actively supported the Hitler regime, others spoke out against it, but many assented by silence. Pope Pius XI's 1933 Concordat with Hitler made a deal that Roman Catholics would refrain from being political and the Hitler government would not interfere with public worship and would respect Catholic property. The agreement could clearly be seen as a deal with the devil, but one of its alarming misunderstandings is that silence is apolitical.

"First they came for the communists . . ."

I have heard sermons in which the pastor made disdainful reference to "government taking our money through taxes" or overtly opposing a federal, state, or local policy or practice. Comments like these may not be thought of as political, but they clearly are. Many clergy who consider it inappropriate for congregations to be involved in politics contacted their members of Congress when they learned that the clergy housing tax exemption might be revoked. Sometimes it is just a matter of whose ox is being gored.

When people say that congregations should not get involved in politics, they are asking the wrong question. Congregations influence society and politics both directly and indirectly, both consciously and unconsciously.

---

20. Martiń Luis Guzmán, *Memoirs of Pancho Villá*, tr. Virginia H. Taylor (Austin: University of Texas Press, 1905), 285.

Imagine the well-meaning Scandinavian Lutheran pastor who enjoins her Minnesota congregation to go to the polls and vote for "the best candidate, regardless of political party." Fair enough and nonpartisan. But which of these persons are they most likely to vote for: Justina Gudelyte, Christina Olson, Batchimeg Sambalkhundev, Dovilė Jokubauskienė, or Tebogo Gareitsanye (my former students)? Religious individuals and their congregations cannot escape involvement.

- Whether congregations are taxed or tax exempt is a political decision and states a particular alignment between organized religion and governments.

- Congregations expect to receive public services such as police, fire, and EMT protection but many do not contribute toward the costs. If you withdrew those protections, their political character would suddenly be laid bare.

- Religious groups are subject to zoning laws, sanitation, and other laws that are formulated and enforced through the political process.

- Courts sometimes order medical treatment of children for life-threatening diseases even though the parents hold religious beliefs that proscribe such treatment. Children are sometimes removed from homes even though the parents claim that their punishment of the child is religiously sanctioned.

- During the pandemic, governments decided that public well-being required congregations to forgo public worship.

- The church where I grew up had the United States flag on one side of the altar and the Christian flag on the other and did lots and lots of "flag waving."

- Some of us earned the *Pro Deo et Patria*, For God and Country, award in the church-sponsored Boy Scout troop.

The question is not whether congregations are involved in politics, but how they are engaged. Whether people choose to articulate the connection with politics and policy, those implications are clearly there in the texts, hymns, sermons, rituals, and education programs. Congregations are about, among other things, values, moral socialization, and moral guidelines, which have implications at the political as well as the personal level. Since individuals and congregations are already enmeshed in public and therefore political life, what is the character and quality of their engagement? When, how, and who?

Hell Yes, at Dinnertime

Individual families and congregations must decide what works best in their situation because the personal dynamics of each setting are specific. But families and congregations, rooted in an ethos of love and support, are the best places for heated social divisions to be addressed, as long as we don't expect them necessarily to be resolved. They can be places where values are discussed as people try to sort out the meaning of life, personal decisions, and public policies.

This is part of their function as mediating institutions. Careful planning and attention to the things that unite can, in many cases, set the stage for people to learn from one another about their differences.

In 1966, a friend invited me to preach at the congregation on the south side of Chicago where he was the pastor. I ended a gentle, nonconfrontational sermon with, "And so, everyone who has God as his father (sic) has Martin Luther King as his brother." The council summoned the pastor and took away his right to invite supply pastors without their supervision.

Not long after that, my friend left parish ministry and went to work for Lutheran Social Services. In my newfound zeal for the civil rights movement, I had not taken the time to understand people threatened by racial change in their neighborhoods even though the brotherhood premise seemed morally compelling yet innocuous.

The pulpit is a problematic place to address the specifics of controversial political issues because it is one-way, non-dialogical communication. The bulk of a congregation's effort should go into encouraging, educating, and supporting members in their roles as families and citizens. "There is a time to tear, and a time to sew; a time to keep silent, and a time to speak."

Pastors or social activists sometimes rush to congregations or seminaries with causes (those who know me, know I'm talking about myself), but may not have done the strategic homework necessary to understand where people already are, how much they might change views over time, and what it might take to get them to change. And there is always the risk that the change the pastor wants will turn out to be wrong, more complicated than the pastor thinks, or even later judged to be harmful or immoral.

It takes patience and long-term planning to address major social concerns. I once visited a small congregation in Louisiana where a handful of activists said they were going to get the whole congregation involved in Bread for the World's Offering of Letters to Congress. I advised them not to push the church council too hard, because if they got a strong "no," it might block participation for years. If they got turned down, they could at least write their own letters.

When I returned a year later, I asked how it had gone. "Oh, that blankety-blank church council." "But did you write any letters as part of the annual campaign?" "Well, yes, five of us did."

They had arranged for me to teach an adult class on this second visit. At the end of the class, participants were invited to write a letter supporting the policy BFW was advocating. I also invited listeners who disagreed with BFW's recommendations to write or call their member of Congress to oppose BFW's position because participation on both sides was essential to sustaining democracy.

Most members of the class wrote a letter then and there. A year later the whole congregation was participating in the Offering of Letters. It took three years, but change happened. Real change requires long-term planning and, ultimately, a change in the culture of congregations and the seminaries that prepare people for ministry, though seminaries are a story for another day.

Decades ago, a Fort Worth pastor approached me asking for advice on how to deal with a situation that had arisen in his congregation. A gay couple had started attending worship, and one of the partners was a pastor in their denomination. He said that he was okay with them coming but that the congregation was not ready. He was right, the congregation was not ready. But the question was, what was he going to do to get them ready? "Think of it as a multi-year plan. Think of it like you think of a building program, stewardship program, or an educational program. What is your long-term plan to get them ready?"

A few years later, pamphlets and books about homosexuality covered a table near the entrance. Things had changed and have continued to change there, because social acceptance had become an intentional priority, not a residual "when we have time to get to it" or "only when the fires are burning" activity.

When I introduced the United Nations Sustainable Development Goals to a Saturday morning group of congregants in Maryland, people commented that between 50 to 75 percent of their members were not present because they thought the UN was a terrible organization. The congregation was politically divided, much like the rest of society. Here was a situation where it might be possible to mitigate some of the bitterness that divides American political culture.

Under patient leadership, forums could be offered, and in the case of families at dinnertime, structured conversations. People who claim they share the same values could begin by sharing those values, including the values articulated in their religious tradition; learning to listen respectfully to one another like an anthropologist would listen to an indigenous tribe in the Brazilian rainforest; learn why they see things as they do; their personal experiences with the issue at hand; the news sources that lead them to their opinions and why they choose those over others; and over time, seeing why one another have different points of view. Though the differences may remain, they can learn from, and continue to cherish, one another. Civil discourse is important in families, congregations, and political democracy.

Perhaps I am too optimistic and emotional divisions are too strong. But there are groups doing programs of this sort and online resources for anyone who wants to try at the family or congregational level. "Religious and secular groups often exhibit differences when it comes to family planning, and yet groups such as the Faith to Action Network, the United Nations Population Fund, World Vision, and Christian Connections for International Health have worked carefully together to craft areas of agreement, shared strategies, and actions."[21] Too few congregations seem to take this aspect of their public character seriously, and few seminaries apparently have programs that prepare clergy to lead structured programs of this sort, let alone preparation for leading congregations in their calling to citizenship. Congregations can be communities of moral and political discourse and discernment.

Religious people, grounded in long-term human experience of wrestling with life's biggest problems, a utopian vision, and centuries of experience in addressing social ills, have a vital stake in the common good. Stated in the indicative, religious people are involved in politics whether they want to be or not. Stated in the imperative, religious individuals should be involved in public life. Political involvement is a natural expression of the values espoused by religious groups.

Public involvement by congregational members can be a value added. It can also be a value to the congregation itself as it begins to see itself as a public entity in conversation with other public entities. Religious institutions are not merely private institutions. Their public engagement affirms the public character of religious and theological commitments.

We should not run away from the slow but critical task of transforming the culture of congregations, which means we must be there in the first place. Changes can and will happen if approached strategically with politics that are charitable. Sr. Sally Duffy O.S.C. of the SC Ministry Foundation observes that when a parish begins to take social justice seriously, it transforms other aspects of a congregation's life, even in such things as liturgy and Bible study. Congregants not only have a lot to give, but a lot to gain, and the public square can benefit from an infusion of religious values.

We are called to a spiritual vocation to help all people, families, especially the dispossessed, to make advances that sustain and

---

21. Karen Hoehn, "Faith and Family Planning: Working Together to Drive Progress Post-2020," FP2020, October 2019, *http://www.familyplanning2020.org/sites/default/files/Our-Work/CSO/11.01.19_FP2020_Faith_Brief_Final.pdf.*

improve human life for others as well as ourselves. In 1948, just prior to his assassination, Mahatma Gandhi said, "My devotion to truth has drawn me into the field of politics . . . those who say that religion has nothing to do with politics do not know what religion means."[22]

"The Firebird"

> *Our unity must be forged in the fires of solidarity.*
>
> —Aaron Goggans, *Black Lives Matter*

The fire of power burns only the flammable,
united only in the burning sameness
their common vulnerability defines.
Incinerating each in the flame of every,
it feeds its ravenous lust for fuel
with no distinction or name but tinder.

The fire of progress consumes the past.
Kindled in castoff scraps and leaves,
its twigs and wrappers ripped and yellowed,
it burns the stories and limbs and branches
torn from trunks of fir and elm, pine and red oak,
history and heritage, wall and roof-beam and roots.

The fire of resistance burns for justice,
shines the light of Black lives that matter,
of love that is only love, embraces the heat
of tents and prisons where fear discards the fearful.
It welcomes the pain of each broken twig
and gathers it into its own wounded burning self.

---

22. Louis Fischer, ed., *The Essential Gandhi: His Life, Work, and Ideas* (New York: Random House, Vintage Books, 1962), 4, citing M.K. Gandhi, "Farewell," *The Story of My Experiments with Truth* (London: Phoenix Press, 1949), 420.

The fires of power and progress leave ashes,
crumbling gray dust of lives growing cold,
no longer flammable, useful no longer, deported
to slag-heaps, imprisoned in landfills, dead
to producers of profit and privilege. Their stories
and memories dissipate in oily darkling clouds.

From the ashes of resistance, new fire emerges;
in solidarity forged in the flames, a fiery winged creature
arises to life—all black, white, red, yellow, and green;
all yin and yang, all Western and Eastern;
all ancient and modern, faithful and faithless,
female and male and more.

Both Phoenix and Fenghuang, it sings:

We are born again,
We are born again.
The one that is all is born again,
The all that is one is born again.
We are they, they are we,
You are in me and I in you:
I am therefore you,
You are therefore me.
The fire is the Huang,
The Feng is the fire.
Soar then, soar!
Sing for joy! Sing for joy![23]

—Jim Benton

---

23. The song in italics is taken from the poem "The Nirvana of the Feng and Huang" by Guo MoRuo in 1920 and combines attributes of the Chinese *fenghuang* (*feng* suggests male and *huang* suggests female) and the Western phoenix. (Originally published in *Chinese Literature*, 4.1958). The original fifth line is "We are he, they are me."

CHAPTER 9

Spiritual Disciplines

This is what the good guys do.
They keep trying.
They don't give up.

—*The Road*

The Children Were Kinetic Art

Spiritual disciplines are structured methods that help us stay the course, grow in commitment, and become more effective. When we hear the term *spiritual disciplines*, we typically think of prayer, sacrifice, fasting, meditation, and scripture study.

The spiritual disciplines of *We Carry the Fire* are disciplines of social and political engagement: determined, persistent, sacrificial, effective work that enriches families and civic life. "A disciplined political practice is a spiritual practice, rooted in deep conviction. It is rooted in love of place—and love of neighbor. The discipline of sustained political engagement has always been crucial to democracy."[1]

Decades ago, I made a one-time stop between lectures in Winnipeg and my Texas classroom to visit the Minneapolis Institute of Art. It was weekday-empty, quiet, tranquil, and perfect for art appreciation. As I ascended the curving staircase to the second floor, dozens of school buses drove up and disgorged, surely, all the fourth graders in the Twin Cities, as well as their beleaguered teachers, all escaping classrooms for a foretaste of summer freedom. The *New York Times* advises that one of five essential rules for viewing art is: "Start by avoiding noise like the plague." Those noisy kids were going to ruin my chance of a lifetime to view this collection.

---

1. "Editorial," *Christian Century*, March 15, 2017, 7.

I hurried up the staircase to enjoy the art before the kids got there, but the turmoil arrested my attention. The children splashed through the front doors. Vivid red, yellow, green caps and coats bobbed in and out, high-pitched laughter and noisy chatter filled the galleries, along with gleeful energy and bouncing vitality, as though hundreds of screeching parrots, abruptly uncaged, flew chaotically into the separate galleries below.

It dawned on me that this vivacity, these sounds and hues, were kinetic art: moving sculptures, a dazzling squiggly living canvas. So, as I moved among the galleries, I appreciated the art, the children's reaction to the art, and their reactions to one another. The colorful, noisy aesthetic of excited children made the experience richer. At least four transformations occurred in those fleeting moments.

- I stopped and paid attention.
- I changed my interpretation.
- I shifted emotionally.
- I acted differently.

These steps are familiar spiritual disciplines, ancient and modern. To give just one example, a professor of world religions said that he assigned students a Zen exercise where they were to sit on the ground and look at a patch of grass for at least half an hour. Because they stopped and focused, they would see details not ordinarily seen. The above four transformations are also crucial to the arts and disciplines of social and political spirituality.

The Discipline of Stopping and Noticing

The first step is the choice to rush on or pause and notice. Architects and artists sometimes help us take that step. The entrance to Louis Kahn's Kimbell Art Museum in Fort Worth is structured to shift our attention from our normal way of seeing things to a heightened aesthetic sensitivity.

Along the side, water in a long horizontal pond splashes down over the edge. As you move toward the entrance, you pass through a small grove of trees that Kahn called a "geometrical green room." Sunlight coming through the leaves dapple our bodies and surroundings. Our feet sense the texture of the pebbled walkway that precedes the steps to the lobby. We are invited to notice, to separate ourselves from mundanity, to quicken our senses in preparation for the museum's unique architecture and engaging collection.

The entrance to the Metropolitan Museum of Art in New York invites a different shift in attention. With Central Park as a backdrop, a long flight of stairs between imposing marble lions ascends from the traffic-busy street leading to giant columns that prepare us for grandeur.

To get to the Andy Warhol museum in Pittsburgh, you cross a bridge over the river or negotiate a complicated multi-lane interstate highway. You park in a shadowy area under the bridge, walk through a parking lot, cross a busy street to see an entrance to a seven-story, nearly square, plain building a block from the baseball stadium—urban commonalities of the sort that Warhol noticed and caused us to see in a different way.

Much of modern art helps us see colors, planes, and objects in a fresh way. The Reichstag is a powerful symbol of both the good and evil in German political life. The artists Christo and Jeanne-Claude wrapped the Bundestag, figuratively obscuring its Nazi past, and yet celebrating its future as a surprise package. When the wrapping came off, reconstruction continued, and the capital moved from Bonn to the Reichstag in a new, no longer divided Germany.

Sometimes the coming to awareness moment is thrust upon us. My son Benjamin, genetically Kenyan-Ukrainian, was raised in our otherwise White family. He writes:

> Grades six to ten were terribly confusing. I was living in Wichita Kansas and had what I thought was a best friend. But, when he got upset, he would yell nigger-nigger-nigger until I ran away hurt and

angry. I also had girlfriends, but we had to meet in secret because they feared what their friends would say.

The summer of 1995, between my Associate Degree at Rio Hondo Community College and matriculating at Pomona in the fall, I decided to drive to Fort Worth. Texas had a bad reputation among Blacks. For example, three years later, African American James Byrd Jr. was severely beaten, urinated on, defecated on, chained to a pickup truck, and dragged for three miles; his mutilated, decapitated body abandoned in front of an African American Church. Evidence suggested that he was alive for more than half the dragging.

I had grown up in Texas and was not thinking in racial terms as I entered West Texas. As the day moved on, towns and music stations seemed to get farther apart. A dashboard light signaled I was low on gas, so I pulled into a small dusty station with old-fashioned pumps. I decided to play it safe and pay before pumping. The cashier was at the counter, there were empty spaces where there might once have been racks of food, and four good ol' boys were sitting around a table playing cards.

They glanced my way and one murmured something to the others. He rose, looked me up and down, then straight in the eye, and said "Boy you best git." I knew what could come next, so I spun around, dashed to my car, and got the hell out of there.

My perception of myself and the world changed that day. I recognized sharply for the first time that I was a category, a Black man living in White America and that standards would be different for me. I would always have to be prepared for discrimination and be twice as good as Whites to be successful.

During a summer Research Fellowship at the Medical College of Wisconsin, I shared the West Texas story with other minorities. To my amazement, they were not surprised, only glad that I had been able to go on safely. They had no problem understanding how I had been received.

While growing up, I had been sheltered from, and thus ill prepared for, what it means to be Black in America. I often think about how people of color are urged to adopt children of color so the child can be better equipped for what lies ahead. That being said, I am happy with how I was brought up. I now have two worlds and can fight to reduce the disparities that exist. As I write about my experience a quarter century later, it is clear that we as a nation are not home yet.

In the late 1960s while I was working as a chaplain at Chicago's Navy Pier, a sailor from a Nigerian freighter asked directions to a residence on the South Side. A longshoreman from the docks had invited him to come and party. I tried to explain, "Take the bus to this stop, and then transfer to that one, and get off at this place," but realized it was too confusing, and that the address was between the Pier and Hyde Park where I lived, so told him we would drop him off.

We discovered that the "residence" was actually an apartment in the high-rise Robert Taylor homes, notorious for poverty, violence, and narcotics, described as "stairwells . . . controlled by drug gangs. Robbery, rape, and murder were commonplace." I was scared. As we walked toward the building, a housing authority guard happened upon us and thought it best to accompany us. We took the crowded elevator to the eighth floor, traversed a crappy corridor, knocked, and asked for the longshoreman.

"No, never heard of the guy," she said.

It could only mean trouble when a foreign-looking Black, a White thirty-two-year-old (social worker? plainclothes police officer?), and a housing security guard showed up at her door at night. What is it like to live in such fear when someone knocks on your door?

"No, never heard of the guy," she said. We explained.

"Let me check," she said and closed the door. Moments later, she invited the Nigerian in. The next day he told me that they partied all night.

When we stop and pay attention, we see many things, not just one. New seeing shifts the shape of our experience, makes it plural, deeper, richer. We learn more about the varieties of the human spirit. During 2020 when people became isolated due to COVID-19, many were forced to stop and noticed fresh things about themselves, other people, and social life that normally remained unseen because they were taken for granted.

In John Cage's composition "4'33'''" the pianist sits down to play, and four and a half minutes of silence ensue. People say, "We came to hear music," "Why sit in a concert hall to hear silence?" The silence is "an act of *framing*, of enclosing environmental and unintended sounds in a moment of attention to open the mind to the fact that all sounds are music"—when you're outdoors, the song of a bird, the rush of the wind and indoors, the shuffling of feet, a patron's cough.[2]

In *Anil's Ghost*, Michael Ondaatje writes, "The forest was so still that Anil heard no sounds until she thought of listening for them. Then she located the noisemakers in the landscape, as if using a sieve in water, catching the calls of orioles and parrots."[3]

The first spiritual discipline is to choose to stop and examine taken-for-granted social and political realities, unexamined beliefs, and assumptions. The stimulus in the museum came from outside, but sometimes the change of noticing comes from within. We choose to focus on the trees, the path, then the birds and squirrels, then the ferns and flowers, the sky filtering through the wind-blown leaves, and then again, the scene as a whole.

Noticing is essential—in our social relationships, on the street outside, in political life, and especially in the places where people suffer. Choosing to notice is spiritual noticing when we tune into specific expressions of the human spirit and how they are ennobled or degraded.

An article in the *New Yorker* described someone saying that he had become aware that as he went about his days, he took for granted the benefits of a political system that other people worked so hard to

---

2. Kyle Gann, *No Such Thing as Silence: John Cage's "4'33",* Yale, quoted in Alex Ross, "Searching for Silence: John Cage's Art of Noise," *New Yorker,* October 4, 2010, *https://www.newyorker.com/magazine/2010/10/04/searching-for-silence.*

3. Michael Ondaatje, *Anil's Ghost* (New York: Random House, Vintage International, 2000), 189.

ensure. He was not contributing. He described himself as a "free rider," enjoying the benefits but not contributing to the cost. He added, "Next time I see an injustice, I'm going to speak out."

That is not good enough. We cannot wait until we see an injustice. It is all around us all the time, but because we do not stop to notice, we do not see discrimination, the wider effects of our spending or consumption patterns, the daily situation of impoverished people. How deprived our lives are if we do not step outside the borders of our comfortable daily existence and experience broader expressions of the human spirit. Our souls are continuously enlarging or shrinking.

Henri Matisse's pen and ink sketch *Mlle. Antoinette Seen in Profile to the Right, Wearing a Plumed Hat* shows his model Antoinette's face in profile, her eyes, nose, and ears obscured behind the great plumes of her hat. Only her mouth is visible. She speaks but does not hear, see, or even notice her surroundings. Stunted social spirituality. She's too busy showing off her hat to engage with the world around her.

The Discipline of Changing Interpretation

The second transformation in the museum was a changed interpretation, a mental or cognitive shift. I began to interpret the children's activities through a different frame of reference. Whereas at first they were a noisy interruption, they became a delight—the joyful wildness of the human spirit let loose, a vivacious blessing.

Our assumptive frames of reference, the assumptions embedded in our ways of seeing the world, are powerful and mysterious because they lie behind everyday seeing, our interpretation, our actions. It is as though we view the world through a picture frame or window. We only see what the frame allows. It structures our seeing, lets us see this but not that. The glass in the frame has a color that allows us to perceive things in this color or that.

We sit in a theater and watch an actor being murdered onstage. It looks as though someone is being killed right before our eyes, but our interpretive frame of reference assures us that there will be no blood.

Our frame of reference tells us that we need not call 911 and rush forward to restrain the murderer and aid the victim.

A *New York Times* ad features a female model carrying a pink purse with a teacup puppy peering out between the handles. The woman and the puppy stare at us. It shouts "RALPH LAUREN." We do not have to stop and figure out whether Ralph is the name of the woman, the purse, or the dog, because our enculturated frames of reference tell us that Ralph is the name of a fashion designer. We take it for granted, but someone from a markedly different culture might think Ralph is the name of the dog, or even the woman.

During the Crusades, the battles dragged on so long that sometimes opposing sides came to know one another. Arab Scholar Beha ad-Din wrote, "At times people would sing and others would dance, so familiar had they become over time, and then after a while they would revert to fighting."[4] They shifted their interpretation for a brief time, like the opposing forces in World War I that climbed out of their trenches to sing Christmas songs together. Interpretation matters, is a shape shifter, and when it does, it controls understanding and can change behavior.

Frames of reference make it difficult for people to find common ground. Two people may look at the same event, but they see different aspects and interpret it differently. They listen to different sources of news, which push them to interpret events in vastly different ways. My real news is seen as fake news by someone else.

The museum encounter was accidental, but we can also choose to reinterpret the meaning of events, other people, and our world by choosing to try on a new, or widen an old, frame of reference. Attempt to see the world as the "other" sees it. Social spirituality nurtures and celebrates people whose frame of reference we share, but also steps outside our taken-for-granted frames of reference to understand the frame of reference of the stranger, the other, the opponent, and especially the

---

4. Quoted in Jonathan Phillips, *Holy Warriors: A Modern History of the Crusades* (New York: Random House, 2009), 144.

dispossessed. Congregations provide a value-based frame of reference that can help us do that.

Moral and Spiritual Interpretation

In spiritual discernment, we first see the world in ordinary, everyday, taken-for-granted reality, then choose to dive deeply into its vivacity, complexity, beauty, goodness, and evil, including its transmundane, transcendent, more-than dimension—the goodness and beauty of latent possibilities for things to be better. Spiritual discernment entails seeing the potential spiritual power of goodness in the everyday, feeling its presence, understanding the direction it is moving, and becoming part of that movement for good.

It also calls us to see the harmful and immoral side of the human experience. William James quotes Victorian thinker John Ruskin:

> If suddenly . . . in the midst of . . . a London dinner-party, the walls of the chamber were parted, and through their gap the nearest human beings who were famishing and in misery were borne into the midst of the company feasting and fancy free; if, pale from death, horrible in destitution, broken by despair, body by body they were laid upon the soft carpet, one beside the chair of every guest,— would only the crumbs of the dainties be cast to them; would only a passing glance, a passing through, be vouchsafed to them? Yet the actual facts . . . are not altered . . . by the few feet of ground (how few!) which are, indeed, all that separate the merriment from the misery.[5]

The following list intends no disrespect for the 3,000 victims of 9/11, many of whom were unimaginably brave. Let me say it again, unimaginably brave. Thousands of children in other parts of the world died that very same day from conditions related to malnutrition. But

---

5. William James, *Essays on Faith and Morals* (New York: New American Library, Meridian Books, 1962), 6–7.

we interpret this gross immorality as normal everyday stuff. Heroic people interpreted 9/11 as a disaster and rushed to help, as they should have. But, when it came to malnutrition:

Victims: 24,000 children

Where: poor countries

Special televised programing: 0

Newspaper articles: 0

Messages from the president: 0

Acts of solidarity: 0

Public minutes of silence: 0

Public victim mournings: 0

Organized forums: 0

Papal messages: 0

Alert level: 0

Army mobilization: 0[6]

Albert Schweitzer advised: "Think occasionally of the suffering of which you spare yourself the sight." One advantage (and disadvantage) of working in a poverty or environmental nonprofit is that you never forget the actualities and potentialities of human suffering as well as visions of hopeful change.

Community organizers emphasize the importance of listening to people, and some describe it as a spiritual discipline. It is a discipline because we have to intentionally take time away from other things. It takes effort, attention, focus, and practice to discern the souls of those who suffer most, whether families close at hand or members of the human family who are remote from your daily life.

Jan Chozen Bays, a pediatrician and Zen teacher, writes with humorous self-deprecation:

---

6. Adapted from *http://library.thinkquest.org/25009/results/results.malnutrition.html*, a site closed in 2013.

As we sit (doing meditation), visions of spiritual orphans float through our heads. We picture our child wandering through the neighborhood, dirty in an unironed shirt, thumb in his mouth. Someone says, "Where's your mommy?" "My mommy is getting enlightened." She observes that "being pregnant . . . seeing my kid off to school . . . soapy dish water" are all parts of the enlightened way, "parts of our Buddha self."[7]

Quite so, but suppose that while you were meditating, your three-year-old strayed into a busy intersection. Wouldn't you jump up and do something? Whether your child was saved, hurt, or killed would shape your future actions as well as meditations. Many children are dying today, but for the most part we are busy meditating. Don't bother us with climate change. Don't bother us with potential pandemics. We need that new gas-guzzling car, not higher taxes to prepare for dangers that lie ahead. The way you interpret your place in the world of everyday life shapes how you think and act.

Harvard theologian Gordon Kaufman's Ferguson Lectures at Manchester University in the UK include a challenge to how we normally interpret both everyday life and theology:

> I have focused on the significance of the possibility of nuclear holocaust for the reorientation of Christian theology. When one puts the matter that way, it may seem that I have trivialized to an extreme the enormity of the event we are considering: in the face of such a potential catastrophe, who could care about such things as recasting theology? The disproportion is so great as to be comic. . . . It is obvious that political and moral imperatives of the most urgent sort are here laid upon us all. We must work with far greater effectiveness toward stopping the nuclear arms race, and indeed, toward total nuclear disarmament.[8]

---

7. Jan Chozen Bays, "Taking Realization into Everyday Life," *Mountain Record*, Winter 1987–88, 13–16.

8. Gordon D. Kaufman, *Theology for a Nuclear Age* (Manchester, UK: Manchester University Press/The Westminster Press, 1985), 14.

Lewis B. Puller Jr.'s father was the most decorated Marine in U.S. history. Puller, who lost one hand, fingers of the other, and large parts of both legs in the Vietnam War, wrote a Pulitzer-winning biography, *Fortunate Son*, in which he recalled an incident while recovering from his wounds.

Outside his hospital room window there were boisterous noises of traffic shuttling spectators to and from the John F. Kennedy Memorial Stadium for the Army-Navy game, and I could not reconcile the differing circumstances of the mob outside with the suffering of my platoon back in Vietnam. It seemed insane that men I knew should be groveling in the mud of being blown to bits while most of America was concentrating on point spreads.[9]

For the most part, we live out our daily lives in blind and benign interpretations of what's important while millions of people's hair is on fire. Disaster is part of the everyday lifestyle of those who suffer most. It seems to evince mass compassion only when it is sudden, large scale, and especially when it affects us.

We were surprised when the COVID-19 pandemic hit, yet Laurie Garrett had published *The Coming Plague* in 1994, more than a quarter of a century earlier. We thought we had more pressing things to think about. Our interpretation of what was important did not include spending time working for candidates who would support preparation for pandemics and more adequate health care systems.

Former senator Sam Nunn told a story about a reporter during the conflict in Sarajevo. A little girl had been shot in the head. The reporter helped the man holding the child carry the child to the reporter's car. They sped toward the hospital and the man holding the child urged, "Hurry, my friend, my child is still alive." A bit later, "Still warm," then "Getting cold." The child died.

---

9. Lewis B. Puller Jr., *Fortunate Son: The Autobiography of Lewis B. Puller Jr.* (New York: Bantam Books, 1991), 208.

As the two men were in the lavatory, washing the blood off their hands and their clothes, the man turned to the reporter and said that he now had to perform the terrible task of telling the child's father. The reporter was amazed. He looked at the grieving man and said, "I thought she was your child." The man looked back and said, "No, but aren't they all our children?" And Nunn went on to say, "Yes they are all our children."[10] It is all in how you interpret what you see.

A moral frame of reference invites us to focus our attempts on understanding the people who are less fortunate and the big-picture threats to all our existence. Our personal habits frame of reference invites us to look at the wider connections of our activities—how we use our time, and the wider social and political implications of how we spend our money. A spiritual lens invites us to ask, What can I do to raise the quality of the human spirit—both mine and others? What is the possibility for goodness, more beauty, in this situation? Or, how is the human spirit degraded if I look the other way and fail to act? An empathic frame of reference invites us to remember that they are all our children.

Political Interpretation

The discipline of political interpretation adds an extra layer. You need to know not only what's wrong or potentially dangerous, but must think about what could be done about it on a scale that makes a difference—to make a personal, political, and/or policy connection with actual and potential suffering. Politics cannot address every sort of human suffering, but it is possible to see how widespread suffering can often be addressed, public well-being safeguarded, and humanity enriched through public policies.

The New Deal was a response to the Great Depression. Civil and other human rights laws are a response to violations of human rights.

---

10. Washington, DC, February 1, 1996. Senator Nunn's comments appeared in *Washington Post*; he gave permission to use them in an annual report on world hunger that I was supervising at Bread for the World Institute.

Traffic laws rise out of human suffering and are written to prevent that suffering. Thousands of deaths probably could have been prevented during the pandemic if the right political decisions had been made and helpful preventative steps taken. The list is as long as there are policies and laws—alcohol and other drugs, education, environment, personal violence, property rights, international diplomacy—which is why, when it comes to politics, it is crucially important to funnel your energy through political parties and advocacy groups that specialize in having appropriate information and are doing something about your concerns.

The Discipline of Altering Emotions

The way we interpret situations can powerfully influence how we feel about them. "Your friend committed suicide: no, she was murdered" changes not only the way we interpret what happened, but how we feel about it. The experience in the art museum brought about a shift from anticipation to annoyance to appreciation, from disappointment to delight. Emotional responses change over time and in different contexts.

Social and political spirituality call for sympathy—compassion for the other, and empathy; standing toward the other whether it is someone close at hand or far away. "The heart possesses, within its own realm, a strict analog of logic, which it does not, however, borrow from the logic of the intellect."[11] Love and sympathy have moral value because they evidence a measure of transcendence of "me-only" egocentrism, allowing us to feel beyond our own needs and immediate interests.

I showed Don McCullin's photographs from *Hearts of Darkness*[12] to seminary students. There are stark scenes of human suffering. We

---

11. Max Scheler, *The Nature of Sympathy*, trans. Peter Heath, intro. W. Stark (Hamden, CT: Shoestring Press, Archon Books, 1970), 3.

12. Don McCullin, *Hearts of Darkness*, intro. John Le Carré (New York: Random House, 1981).

wince at the distraught Turkish woman who is about to cover the blood-soaked body of her husband sprawled on the floor, killed in the Cypriot civil war. A nine-year-old Vietnamese boy with napalm scarred tissue curving around his ear and mouth, down his neck and chest, stares at the camera, and us.

A Bangladeshi father gently lays the body of his cholera-stricken nine-year-old son alongside a one-year-old infant in the dead body compound of a refugee camp. A mother, not yet willing to give up her dead baby, cradles it as she "walks relentlessly" around the camp.

Biafran children hold empty cans as they stand in line waiting for food. The photographer notes that they were later driven away by soldiers. What is so striking is not just their ribs outlined by taut skin, but the vacant, listless look in their eyes. They don't even have the energy to be angry.

A picture described as "Biafran soldier rushing wounded comrade from the front" shows a boy, maybe sixteen, carrying a maybe thirteen-year-old boy on his back. "Soldiers," it says. Photos of urban vagrants on the streets of London. In Africa, an African albino child, near death from starvation—his legs so thin they cannot hold his weight, suffers ridicule as well as starvation. A mentally handicapped sixteen year old clutches a metal bowl that looks like a hospital bedpan, extends his other hand begging for food.

Newsweek brought attention to the book with a picture captioned, "Madonna and Child." A startlingly emaciated twenty-four-year-old African mother—the age of my students—sits on a bed, the edges of her mouth slightly turned down, sad, resigned, staring somberly with a slight hint of defiance, straight at us. An infant sitting on her lap grasps and tries to suck from a breast that hangs down to the woman's belly button like wet tissue paper.

Tears were an appropriate, genuinely human response. But many students instead got angry. "I don't want to see it," they said. "I already know about it." But did their knowing lead to doing anything about similar situations that occur on an everyday basis somewhere in the world? Many people avoid places where they see painful things.

Perhaps their own personal pain is so great that they cannot afford additional pain. Or perhaps they are afraid to face reality.

We need not only to see things we do not want to see, but to allow ourselves to feel them deeply. We need to go to the places where suffering exists. Otherwise, we are choosing to be blind to realities of the human spirit. Reality affects real people whether we like it or not, whether we allow it into our lives or not. They are us by another name.

Philosopher Richard Rorty says, "We should raise our children to find it intolerable" that the gap between those who are paid large salaries, including most of us, and "people who get their hands dirty cleaning our toilets, and a hundred times as much as those who fabricate our keyboards in the Third World. . . . Our children need to learn, early on, to see the inequalities . . . as neither the Will of God nor the necessary price for economic efficiency, but as an evitable tragedy."[13]

Rorty says, "evitable," preventable, not "inevitable." He says that the foundation of our moral obligation lies in our ability to be sensitive to the pain of other people, "whether they are of the same family, tribe, colour, religion, nation or intelligence as oneself." And, that the essence of religious faith is the exercise of the moral imagination expressed in love and hope for the human community that makes us "willing and able to treat the needs of all human beings with the respect and consideration with which we treat the needs of those closest to us, those whom we love."[14]

The Discipline of Changing How We Act

Cognitive-behavioral therapy suggests that what we think about something affects both how we feel and potentially what we do about it. The museum experience led to a shift in action. I slowed down because I had more to see. I changed what I looked at, and the

13. Richard Rorty, *Philosophy and Social Hope* (London: Penguin Books, 1999), 203.
14. Ibid., 14, 79, 160, 202–3.

experience forever changed museum-going. Now, museums are always an experience of art-and-people appreciation.

Some popular spiritualities say that their disciplines will lead to action, but how often does it lead to action that helps other people? They may talk about doing something, as we do with New Year's resolutions, but the enthusiasm wanes. When we leave retreats, normalcy quickly reestablishes itself, because it has tenure. We are caterpillars who prefer the known comforts of the chrysalis to the harsh unknown dangers of butterfly flight.

When we fail to act on our intentions, we miss the part of spirituality that changes things, the most important and fulfilling part because it reaches beyond our immediate personal feelings and acknowledges the importance of the other. Why not begin with action to be sure that you get there, rather than hope that maybe your spirituality will get to it later?

There are many kinds and qualities of action. You can worship at an altar, get married at an altar, hide from an enemy behind an altar, dance on an altar, have sex on an altar, kill on an altar. So, what is at stake is not just doing something, but doing good, acting morally, and creating beauty in our social and political life. And that requires a moral frame of reference—a social (family) and political (citizen) spirituality.

We influence and are influenced by others in varying degrees. Even the smallest interaction, such as passing someone on the street, at some level reinforces the sense that it is usually safe to pass by others on the street—or, during the COVID-19 pandemic, unsafe. It is a dialogical relationship that flows reflexively back and forth in complex nuances, shifting impacts, starting and stopping like conversation. When we have more extensive contact with another person, as in child rearing or treating the victims of an illness, our influence is magnified in and through them.

Influence moves in ever reflexive circles, because while we are influencing one another directly, the larger society and culture are at every moment shaping us. Society and culture, the elephants in the room, continuously influence our personalities, institutions, and values, usually below the level of conscious awareness. It is our task, our calling to do what we can, along with others, to help shape the fluxing larger forces in the light of moral values.

The sum of our interactions influences the shape of society and, in the long term, culture. When we band together in associations that mediate between individuals and larger institutions such as governments, the part we play may be small, but the sum of our many parts joined in solidarity can be powerful and lasting.

When it comes to politics, most people only bother to show up to vote, if then. It can be a pain in the ass to join and contribute to a group working for families and social justice, intimidating to testify at a hearing or personally lobby your legislator. It takes discipline to hang in there, discipline to attend meetings where there is always at least one dysfunctional person who impedes group processes. It is hard to knock on door after door on behalf of an issue or candidate, only to face rejection or worse. A guy once came to the door with a gun pointed at me.

Yet, the disciplines of our social and political life can be mighty as well as moral. They change history because those who show up and volunteer again and again are a worldwide spiritual group that carries the fires out of which the future will be forged. These disciplines enrich our lives, the lives of those who share our brief moment in history, as well as those who will follow us on whatever remains habitable on Planet Earth. They help fulfill a meaningful spiritual vocation that creates a more humane future.

Nurturing and Caring

The largest amount of nurturing and caring occurs every day as billions of families raise children. There are also acts of caring that rise from peoples' hearts in response to extraordinary circumstances—wars, natural disasters, pandemics, terrorist and criminal attacks. Acts of love. Acts of human solidarity. Profoundly spiritual acts of caring.

When Carole's mother was deep into a terminal illness, Linda—Carole's college roommate from fifty years ago—packed a bag, drove 125 miles, secured a motel room, and took over the night shift at Theresa's bedside to provide a measure of relief for Carole, her sister Deborah, and brother Harold. Linda does this sort of thing for many people.

The *Washington Post* tells the story of a woman who became disabled due to multiple sclerosis. Her husband takes care of her and they have an additional daytime caregiver. In addition, for the past twenty-one years, friends have come in the evening, five nights a week, to give her a massage, help feed her, and talk about their day.

One such person says, "She gives us the inspiration to go on, to overcome anything."[15] People, especially people with religious values and commitments, are doing this sort of thing all the time—caring for children and adults who are unable to care for themselves. Jim Rurak's story of caring for his dying father and helping bathe his increasingly disabled mother, told in the context of sharing the rosary with them, is an example of tales, too many to tell, that rarely make the news.[16]

> Today, more than one in five Americans (21.3 percent) are caregivers having provided [unpaid] care to an adult or child with special needs at some time in the past 12 months. This totals an estimated 53.0 million adults in the United States . . . 26% are caring for someone with Alzheimer's disease or dementia.[17]

Caring for a member of your family can be incredibly difficult, and all who do it deserve a special place of honor. Families are the first, and most important, line of caring for those who suffer. Charities, often with help from government funds, are the second line of

---

15. Allison Klein, "21 years of devotion for Harriet's Harem," *Washington Post,* December 13, 2017, B-2.

16. James A. Rurak, *The Rosary: A Tract for Catholic Misfits* (Eugene, OR: Wipf and Stock Publishers, 2020), 7.

17. AARP Public Policy Institute, "Caregiving in the United States 2020. *https://www.aarp.org/ppi/info-2020/caregiving-in-the-united-states.html.*

defense, and public institutions the last, though necessary resort when problems are too widespread and charitable efforts too limited.

"According to the Centers for Disease Control and Prevention (CDC), there are approximately 15,600 nursing homes in the United States with 1.7 million licensed beds, occupied by 1.4 million patients."[18] More than two-thirds of those homes are for-profit. The owners are probably in it at least partly for the money, which may account for low staffing and standards, and why so many people in nursing homes died during the pandemic. But the staff, though typically underpaid, are often doing the best they can to care for their patients.

Charity

American individuals, bequests, foundations, and corporations gave an estimated $427.71 billion to U.S. charities in 2018. Giving to religion, education, and public-society benefit organizations was down, while giving to international affairs, environmental, and animal organizations was up from the previous year.[19]

Many people turn to Maimonides's "Eight Levels of Charity" to decide how to prioritize their charitable impulses. The lowest level is "unwilling giving," whereas the highest level is to enter into partnership with the person in need "in order to strengthen his hand until he need no longer be dependent upon others."

We should all contribute money and time to nonprofit charities, but also to advocacy groups and political campaigns. It takes discipline on the part of givers, who may have to sacrifice something else to contribute toward political candidates that reflect their values and interests. An elderly member of a women's Roman Catholic religious order once gave up cable access so that she could contribute that money to Bread for the World's education and political efforts to end hunger.

---

18. Kali in Waltham, MA, "Nursing Homes in America," Care.com, January 25, 2019, *https://www.care.com/c/stories/15840/nursing-homes-in-america/* (accessed October 29, 2020).

19. *Giving USA 2019: The Annual Report on Philanthropy for the Year 2018*, June 18, 2019, *https://givingusa.org/giving-usa-2019-americans-gave-427-71-billion-to-charity-in-2018-amid-complex-year-for-charitable-giving/*.

Service

"Currently, 63 million Americans volunteer about 8 billion hours of their time and talent to improve people's lives and the natural world. . . . (valued at) approximately $197.5 billion"[20] Congregations and charities regularly send Americans abroad to serve for a week or up to a lifetime. And staff in many domestic nonprofits, alongside teachers, nursing aides, technicians, and other service workers, whether secular or religious, work for wages much below what they could get elsewhere because they feel a calling to help. They get a sense of meaning by helping other people, especially people who are disadvantaged.

Dag Hammarskjöld, former secretary-general of the United Nations, said: "I inherited a belief that no life was more satisfactory than one of selfless service to your country—or humanity. This service required lifelines of courage to stand up unflinchingly for your convictions."[21]

General Stanley McChrystal, who led U.S. forces in Afghanistan, advocates wider adoption of at least a year of national service, similar to AmeriCorps, the Peace Corps, Teach for America, or the many volunteer programs offered by religious groups. He argues that "We have allowed the obligations of citizenship to narrow."[22] The inalienable rights spoken of by the founders of the country need to be accompanied by inalienable responsibilities.

We can engage in a service project that puts us directly in touch with disadvantaged people while helping them. When we volunteer at a soup kitchen, we don't just ladle out soup. We seek out the recipients who are interested in talking and chat with them like we would chat

20. *Giving USA 2018: Americans Gave $410.02 Billion to Charity in 2017, Crossing the $400 Billion Mark for the First Time,* June 13, 2018, *https://givingusa.org/tag/giving-usa-2018/.*

21. From the radio speech "This I Believe" by Dag Hammarskjöld, 1954, in K. Falkman, *To Speak for the World: Speeches and Statements by Dag Hammarskjöld* (Stockholm: Atlantis, 2005), 58.

22. Stanley McChrystal, "Step Up for Your Country," *Newsweek,* January 31, 2011, 36–39.

with someone we know. They are just another version of ourselves who happen to have had a different set of opportunities, experiences, and biographical narrative.

More than 75,000 people participate in the AmeriCorps program each year, Senior Corps has about 400,000 members nationwide, and 187,000 men and women have joined the Peace Corps and served in 139 countries. They have worked on such things as AIDS education, information technology, and environmental preservation, though some have been recently pulled out of China when we most need bicultural understanding.

In the late 1960s, retired businessman John Van Hengel started the first food bank, St. Mary's Food Bank in Phoenix, Arizona. A food bank is a place where food is gathered and stored to be distributed to food pantries and soup kitchens. Today, the nonprofit Feeding America is the nation's second largest charity, measured by revenue, and networks with 200 food banks that feed 46 million people.

Most of the volunteers in charitable food banks, pantries, and kitchens are motivated by their religious commitments. People of all faiths deliver Meals on Wheels to seniors who are at risk of hunger and carry out volunteer activities such as helping seniors with their taxes through AARP. Students hold hunger fasts on campuses, and there are CROP hunger walks in every state. Individual acts can cumulate in positive results when institutions are supportive.

Howard University reported that in their first year of campus-wide recycling, 11.48 tons of aluminum, glass, and plastic and almost 190 tons of paper products were diverted from waste disposal to recycling. Recycling is a doable activity for millions of people to contribute toward a sustainable future. It is not enough to guarantee that future, but people do participate, even when it is sometimes inconvenient.

Multiply these efforts by billions of people in the U.S. alone—breast cancer walks, environmental group activities, tutoring and mentoring programs—and you begin to get a sense of people's commitment to volunteer service, bringing goodness to others in need. When New York called for volunteers to help with the COVID-19 crisis, 90,000 retired and active health care workers signed up, even though they knew it might increase their chance of becoming infected.

The story of charity and volunteer service fills many books and the hearts of many people. There are multiple ways to participate and thousands of places where you can plug in as an individual. Unleash your passion for service, and discover the surplus of meaning, the enhanced spirituality, you will experience, if (big IF) you hang in and make it a spiritual discipline, not just drop-in-and-out 7-11 public service or in-and-out politics. It becomes a spiritual discipline when you go that extra mile.

Our primary focus here is not about volunteering and charity, nor about the important role the private sector also plays, but the less obvious task of carrying the fire in our public life—giving public voice to the vision of a better world and changing laws and policies and practices for the good of all.

Charitable Politics

A charitable politics combines the heart, the compassion, and the desire to serve, typical of charity with thoughtful, hard-headed strategies and the long-haul resolve of politics. Doing politics is difficult. Max Weber described it as "a slow and difficult drilling of holes into hard boards." It requires discipline to make the sacrifices. If you think the "other side" is wrong or should not have won an election, then it is up to you to double and triple your educational, financial, and advocacy efforts to win. That is the burden and gift of democracy.

"Philosophers have hitherto only interpreted the world in various ways; the point is to change it."[23] At the end of the day we either try to change things for the better or sit back and hope that those who are the movers and shakers have our best interests at heart. Good luck with that.

---

23. Karl Marx, *Theses on Feuerbach* (Stuttgart: Verlag von J. H. W. Dietz, 1888).

When I was a seminary professor, we began the academic year with a Faculty Retreat—that is, we "retreated" to the second-floor coffee lounge. I suggested to the dean that we spent too much time retreating, so the next year he called it the Faculty Advance. After that year's "Advance," I asked what advances we had made. His answer came the third year when he called it the Faculty Focus. The Faculty Focus consisted mostly of the dean's thoughtful, but labored, state of the seminary address. I gave up attempting to get the "retreat-advance-focus" named right. He was trying, though changing the name of something rarely gets you all the way to where you need to be.

Retreats and focusing are good. Advances require more discipline. The previous chapters suggest ways that other people have engaged in local political actions. People who hold public office may have the best chance of making positive changes. For most of us, it means supporting those who run for office by becoming involved with a political party, and/or becoming active in an advocacy group that has staff, money, solid values, and a dedicated grassroots membership.

There are many great such organizations. I use Bread for the World (BFW), which responds to national policies, and affiliates of the Industrial Areas Foundation (IAF), which respond at the local level as examples simply because I know them best. But there are hundreds, if not thousands, of competent and effective groups that focus on the environment, civil liberties, gender, disabilities, education, health, democracy, animals, and on and on—organizations that are reputable, dedicated, informed, and effective, that can help you realize your family and citizen spirituality.

How do they work? BFW has organizers who travel to local areas to educate people about policies that affect hungry and poor people, and empower them to write letters and emails, make phone calls, and visit their members of Congress in organized advocacy campaigns.[24]

---

24. For a review of the effectiveness of calls, emails, and letters, see Kathryn Schultz, "Call and Response," *New Yorker*, March 6, 2017, 26–32, *http://www.newyorker.com/ magazine/2017/03/06/what-calling-congress-achieves*.

They have policy experts who keep in touch with, and attempt to influence, members and staff on Capitol Hill.

The communications staff write and disseminate timely educational and advocacy materials, do public relations campaigns, and help local people learn how to write opinion editorials and deal with local media. The church relations staff work with congregations and denominations. The Institute produces educational programs and materials because it is important that you do not just react, but know what and why you are doing it. And of course, there are tech, administrative, and fundraising staff. You need money to make this all happen.

Gas up the pilot light in your heart about the concerns that engage your passion, and you will find a political party or advocacy organization that helps bring change to the issues that engage those passions. That fire will breathe into your heart, mind, and spirit.

"This little fire of mine, I'm gonna let it shine." You may have to rearrange some of the furniture in your soul, but sing it, shout it, do it.

"The Secret"

The secret of doing anything
every day
is not the dogged determination
of willpower.

It is forgiving yourself
for the days you miss.

The secret of believing in anything
is not the teeth-clenching grit
of stubborn faith.

It is welcoming
the lifegiving energy of doubt.

The secret of everything,
everywhere, all the time,
is not the constant pursuit
of perfection.

It is celebrating
the relentless possibility of hope.

—*Jim Benton*

Spiritual Disciplines of Public Life

	Knowledge	Lifestyle	Congregation	Politics
First Step	• Learn from suffering communities • Keep current with reputable news • Study a policy problem	• Include policy concerns in your devotional life • Consume less, upgrade your diet, conserve energy at home • Give to charitable organizations	• Study your congregation's personnel and consumption practices • Explore social policies and programs in your tradition	• Register and vote • Contribute funds to effective advocacy and political organizations and campaigns • Write letters and emails, make phone calls as part of campaigns
A Little More	• Join an activist organization • Attend public policy events • Learn how the political process works	• Make changes consistent with your values • Be a regular volunteer • Organize fundraisers	• Include concerns in worship/study • Lead children/youth events • Democratize congregational practices	• Become active in neighborhood, city, or state organization • Be actively involved in political campaigns
Still More	Share knowledge with • family • friends • neighbors • at work • school • community groups	• Deepen personal, organizational, lifestyle changes • Recruit other people to activities	• Facilitate local awareness and activities, such as charity walks • Help other congregations organize for advocacy	• Become an advocacy group leader • Meet with policy makers to share concerns
A Lot More	• Take courses in ethics, economics, politics, policy • Write articles, books	• Join service or advocacy program • Become full-time volunteer or staff	• Help your congregation become a public symbol for families, justice, ecology, democracy	• Become a neighborhood or community organizer • Run for political office

Adapted from "Responses to World Hunger," a Franciscans Communications Center poster, 1976.

Afterword

"ain't done"

poetician say, po*try bird,*
been seeing you all around
starting to see poetry all over the place
ain't that good?

po*try bird say
good enough
ain't done

poetician say, po*try bird,
been seeing poetry everywhere
been writing down how I see
ain't that good?

po*try bird say
good enough
ain't done

poetician say, po*try bird,
been writing best words I can
been showing other folks, too
ain't that good?

po*try bird say
good enough
ain't done

poetician say, po*try bird,
been getting other folks seeing poetry,

writing poetry, sharing poetry
ain't that good?

po*try bird say
good enough
ain't done

poetician say, dang, po*try bird,
when you think I be done?
po*try bird say
when everybody doing it

poetician say
everybody don't want to do it!
po*try bird say
ain't done

—*Jim Benton*

• • •

As I was getting off a tour bus in Kuala Lumpur, I asked our tour guide
if he was able to make an adequate living at being a guide or whether
he also had another job. He said, "Oh, this pays really well. I work as
a guide for six months, and then volunteer at an ecology project in
Kalimantan."

There are people like him all over the world who get up in the
morning to work for peace, justice, and sustainability. We are a spiritual family of activists who do our best to carry the fires of family and
citizenship.

In the Fall of 2015, having completed two pastoral interims, I,
with Michael Kuchinsky, initiated a project on the UN's new set of
2015–2030 Sustainable Development Goals, seventeen social and
economic goals that represent the world's best hope for a peaceful,
plentiful, just, and sustainable world—the human spirit at its best.

The people of 193 nations, all creeds, races, and religions, have committed to work together toward achieving these global goals. At the UN meeting where the goals were affirmed, three dramatic moments stood out:

- President Obama asserted, "All of our nations have work to do, and that includes here in the United States. That's why today I am committing the United States to achieving the Sustainable Development Goals."

- Malala and 193 young people held lanterns representing the signatory 193 countries hope for their future.

- Pope Francis said, "Government leaders must do everything to insure that all can have the spiritual and material means needed to live in dignity and to create and support a family."

I encourage you to view the three-and-a-half-minute video, "The United Nations Sustainable Development Summit: 17 Goals to Transform Our World"[1] to learn more about these goals.

Our volunteer team—which now includes Ekema Anjorin, Kati Miller-Holland, Walter Knausenberger, and Ted Steege—takes the message of the Global Goals to congregations, colleges, seminaries, and other community groups—in person when possible, or remotely by ZOOM and other electronic media. We are convinced that, whether or not you realize it, your life, your family, and your spiritual calling as a citizen already intersect with the Global Goals. You can learn more by connecting with our team and downloading helpful resources at GlobalGoalsCalling.net.

---

1. *https://www.youtube.com/watch?v=89tInECFdQ4&list=PLY9QpmUTY0UThOM9-Bt-pMYSdxYxE1GxlY*.